ADELPHI
Paper • 302

The ASEAN Regional Forum

Contents

Oxford University Press, Walton Street, Oxford OX2 6DP
Oxford New York
Athens Auckland Bangkok Bombay
Calcutta Cape Town Dar es Salaam Delhi
Florence Hong Kong Istanbul Karachi
Kuala Lumpur Madras Madrid Melbourne
Mexico City Nairobi Paris Singapore
Taipei Tokyo Toronto
and associated companies in
Berlin Ibadan

Oxford is a trade mark of Oxford University Press

Published in the United States
by Oxford University Press Inc., New York

© The International Institute for Strategic Studies 1996

First published July 1996 by Oxford University Press for
The International Institute for Strategic Studies
23 Tavistock Street, London WC2E 7NQ

Director: Dr John Chipman
Deputy Director: Rose Gottemoeller

British Library Cataloguing in Publication Data

Data available

Library of Congress Cataloging in Publication Data

ISBN 0-19-829263-5
ISSN 0567-932X

INTRODUCTION

During the Cold War, multilateral security arrangements in the Asia-Pacific region had a mixed record. With one notable exception, they took the form of collective defence underpinned by a major power, usually the United States. From the late 1960s, however, a unique form of multilateralism evolved within South-east Asia. This multilateral undertaking, the Association of South-East Asian Nations (ASEAN), had neither a conventional collective defence nor a collective security function. Although ASEAN was established with regional security against communism very much in mind, its founding declaration made no mention of an overt security role. Over time, however, the Association has assumed a distinctive, albeit limited, security role based on the medium of political dialogue.

ASEAN was established in Bangkok in August 1967 by Thailand, Malaysia, Singapore, Indonesia and the Philippines. Brunei joined the Association in 1984 and Vietnam most recently in July 1995. For its member-states, ASEAN provides a forum for inter-related confidence-building and preventive diplomacy. Within South-east Asia, the Association also fulfils the role of a diplomatic community holding a more or less uniform view on regional security issues. These two roles are interlinked and the external, community function has had a positive impact on ASEAN's internal, confidence-building role.[1]

Following the end of the Cold War, however, and at ASEAN's formal initiative, a new and wider multilateral structure has been created in the Asia-Pacific with a clearly defined security role. ASEAN's primary responsibility for this new venture and institutional development is reflected in its title: the ASEAN Regional Forum (ARF). The first working session of the ARF convened in July 1994 in Bangkok. ASEAN is responsible for organising and chairing the Forum's annual meetings, and for co-chairing its inter-sessional activities. Moreover, the prime model for the ARF is ASEAN's own distinctive, political approach to regional security problems.[2] Thus conspicuously absent from the ARF is any robust provision for addressing the use of force in conflict and conflict resolution. Like ASEAN, the ARF is based on the primacy of foreign ministries, although – again as with ASEAN – defence ministry officials have become increasingly associated with the Forum.

Yet the suitability of transposing the ASEAN model within a wider, more uncertain regional security context, dominated by relations between the major regional powers – the United States,

Japan and China – remains to be seen. The potential for turbulence within that wider context was clearly demonstrated by the tensions caused in 1993–95 with the revelation North Korea's nuclear military potential and, more dramatically, in March 1996 by China's military intimidation of Taiwan in the Taiwan Strait that led the US to display its countervailing resolve.[3]

This Paper examines the provenance and so-far limited experience of the ARF as an extension of ASEAN's model of regional security and assesses its suitability for its declared purpose of enhancing political and security cooperation within the wider Asia-Pacific region. Does the advent of the ARF represent a significant structural adjustment to the post-Cold War security context, or is it little more than a variation on an existing and limited security arrangement? Is a distinctive, as well as an effective, multilateral approach to regional security now evolving in the Asia-Pacific?

Since ASEAN has never explicitly declared or articulated a formal model of regional security, such a model has to be inferred and extrapolated from the Association's nearly three decades of practice and experience. Over this period, the ASEAN model has promoted an exclusively political approach to problems of regional security through multilateral dialogue. ASEAN's practice is based on diplomacy alone, and makes no provision for the institutional enforcement characteristic of models of collective security. Nor does it include formal mechanisms for settling disputes for fear of impairing political relationships. To that extent, the ASEAN model suffers from the defects of its qualities.

I. THE CHANGING REGIONAL SECURITY CONTEXT

The emergence of the ASEAN Regional Forum in July 1994 was both a symptom of, and a response to, changes in the security context in East Asia following the end of the Cold War, and, in particular, of its second phase from the early 1970s onwards. During this second phase, Sino-US strategic priorities in the region had converged in a tacit alliance with the aim of containing the Soviet Union's growing assertiveness in the region as manifested through its communist ally, Vietnam. This convergence of Sino-US interests helped to mitigate the strategic consequences that the ignominious end of the Vietnam War would otherwise have had for the United States and its regional partners. Although some ASEAN members found this new pattern of power unpalatable, they did benefit from it, especially from China's decision to abandon its support for revolutionary movements in South-east Asia.

One notable feature of continuity, however, characterised the new pattern of regional power: Indochina remained a critical point of reference for global rivalry. During the first phase of the Cold War, successive governments in Washington had viewed conflict in Indochina from a strategic perspective that assumed a close link between the regional and global balances of power. The US had identified the revolutionary People's Republic of China (PRC) as the prime agent in East Asia for advancing the expansionist goals of a monolithic international communism, especially after its alliance with the Soviet Union and its intervention in the Korean War, respectively at the beginning and end of 1950. China's support for communist insurgency across its common border with Vietnam confirmed the US belief that interlocking proxies of the Soviet Union were attempting to revise the balance and distribution of power in East Asia to their global advantage. The United States' ill-fated military intervention in Vietnam was a direct result of that belief.[1]

In the early 1970s, Sino-US *rapprochement* directed against Soviet ascendancy paved the way for the US withdrawal from Vietnam since the *raison d'être* for the US presence – containing China in Vietnam – was no longer applicable. Indochina, which had become completely subject to revolutionary communism by the end of 1975, remained nonetheless a locus of conflict and a critical geographic point of reference for both regional and global rivalries. The intra-communist war in Cambodia, precipitated by Vietnam's invasion in December 1978, revealed the extent to which Indochina remained both a regional and a global problem. The United States, in tacit alliance with China, still sought to deny the regional dominance of its Soviet adversary as the deployment of Vietnamese military power that threatened Thailand appeared to strengthen the Soviet Union's influence in East Asia. In the event, the manner and circumstances in which the Cold War came to an end, involving both Soviet–US and Sino-Soviet *rapprochement*, changed the Indochina problem as a regional factor in the global balance of power virtually beyond all recognition.

The Cambodian conflict, on both the global and regional levels, was resolved as a direct result of the Cold War's end. With the benefit of hindsight, the defining moment in the conflict's resolution was the attempt by then Soviet Communist Party General Secretary Mikhail Gorbachev, driven by domestic imperatives, to improve global relationships by disengaging the Soviet Union from regional conflicts.[2] The withdrawal of Soviet material and diplomatic support from Vietnam that occurred from the late 1980s obliged the government in Hanoi to make critical choices; one of which was its decision to end the military intervention in Cambodia. In October 1991 in Paris, the Cambodian conflict was settled through the intervention of the permanent members of the United Nations Security Council (UNSC). The Paris settlement was indicative of the qualitative changes already under way in global relationships. In the same way, the security context in East Asia became subject to fundamental change as well.

In the broader East Asian security context, the Indochina problem had lent definition to related regional and global alignments and maintained the incentive for US military engagement in the region, to the advantage of the ASEAN states. For Washington, the only change in the Indochina problem during the two phases of the Cold War was which particular major adversary required containing, not the stake involved – namely, the prospect of an adverse regional dominance with global consequences. When the Cold War ended, such a prospect no longer obtained. Despite its polarising political effect within South-east Asia and beyond, the Indochina issue had put a number of other regional tensions on hold, above all the disputes over territorial and maritime jurisdiction in the South China Sea in which China was the more formidable protagonist. Paradoxically, the resolution of the Indochina problem not only removed a common focus of conflict for the states that had been ranged in loose coalition against Vietnam and the Soviet Union, but it also undermined a structure of constraint.[3]

That structure of constraint was evident at the global level in Sino-US accommodation over both the unresolved issues of Taiwan and the division of the Korean peninsula, again bolstered by their common interest in containing Soviet assertiveness. With both Sino-Soviet and Soviet–US *rapprochement* after the Cold War, however, the pattern of dominant international alignments that had been sustained for nearly two decades began to unravel. The United States lost its crusading ideological cause abroad while its domestic economic difficulties were reflected in budgetary constraints on military expenditure. The erosion of a long-standing strategic rationale for a major US military deployment in East Asia was accelerated by the disintegration of the Soviet Union in December 1991. Only one month earlier, the US Bush administration, despite its recent triumph in the Gulf War against Iraq, had given up in frustration its attempts to negotiate terms to extend the leases to its military bases in the Philippines, and it had given notice of a complete US withdrawal by November 1992. This termination obliged the US to withdraw its forward military presence back to Japan, with which relations had become exceedingly chequered because of economic tensions.

The consequences of the US military withdrawal from its bases in the Philippines were mitigated to a degree by a memorandum of understanding concluded with Singapore in November 1990. This agreement allowed US naval vessels and aircraft to make greater use of Singapore's military facilities. In January 1992, the two countries reached a further accord that permitted a US military logistics facility to relocate from the Philippines to Singapore. Other similar agreements giving limited US naval access to Indonesian and Malaysian ports highlighted the extent of ASEAN's concern at the degree of flux in the post-Cold War regional distribution of power. Although the ASEAN states had never articulated a common strategic perspective as a basis for defence cooperation, they did share the view that a sustained US forward military deployment would have a stabilising effect on East Asia. The degree of overt support for that deployment was mixed, however, as displayed subsequently in the rejection by Thailand, with Malaysian and Indonesian approval, of a US plan to preposition military supply ships in the Gulf of Thailand. Russia, as the principal successor state to the Soviet Union, was not considered an immediate factor in the regional balance of power, while one of the legacies of the 1941–45 Pacific War was a deep-seated regional aversion to Japan assuming a security role commensurate with its great economic power.[4]

In the meantime, China's remarkable economic growth, with its attendant implications for projecting military power, had been demonstrated by its assertiveness in the South China Sea at Vietnam's expense in March 1988. Moreover, the effect in East Asia of the end of the Cold War had been to confer a unique strategic latitude on China, even though it was unable to take full military advantage of it. China was no longer subject to the hostile attentions of major-power adversaries; they had either diminished in strategic significance or appeared to be in strategic decline. The dominant feature of East Asia's post-Cold War security context was that the balance or distribution of power seemed to have been revised to China's decided advantage, emphasising the vulnerability of lesser regional states.[5]

Singapore's 1990 memorandum of understanding with the United States was one attempt to come to terms with the post-Cold War security context. Even more significant for the region was the impact of Indonesian President Suharto's first visit to China in November 1990 as the two countries re-established diplomatic relations after more than two decades. Suharto had been astounded by the pace and extent of China's economic development, and was apprehensive about the prospect of that development sustaining a regional assertiveness. Thus Indonesia lent its influential support to private discussions within ASEAN to promote a wider framework for security dialogue beyond the limited bounds of the Association itself. There was no consensus in ASEAN for any alternative security arrangement based on collective defence because the member-states shared the view that attempting to confront China would be futile. The concept of an extended security dialogue also attracted Thai support after the end of the Cambodian conflict as the Bangkok government reassessed its security interests. Consequently, the need for such an extended structure to cope with the post-Cold War security context was at the top of the agenda at the ASEAN heads of government fourth summit meeting in Singapore in January 1992. Interestingly, this seminal summit was held just after the US had announced in November 1991 its intended withdrawal from its military bases in the Philippines, and after the disintegration of the Soviet Union in December.

The ASEAN Regional Forum emerged as a consequence of the January 1992 summit as the participants recognised the necessity of looking beyond South-east Asia to cope with the new regional security context. In February 1992, one month after the summit, ASEAN's concerns were realised when China reaffirmed its claim to all the island territories in the South China Sea and, apparently, to all the interjacent waters. In doing so, China effectively made clear its intention to extend its sovereign jurisdiction deep into the heart of South-east Asia.

Multilateralism and the Advent of ASEAN

The mixed record of the Cold War multilateral security arrangements in the Asia-Pacific helps to explain why extending ASEAN's model was the preferred option for post-Cold War regional security.

Two other post-1945 multilateral security enterprises in the Asia-Pacific, both supported by the United States, had foundered for different reasons. These were the Collective Defence Treaty for South-East Asia, concluded in Manila in September 1954 following the temporary settlement of the first Indochina War in Geneva the previous July, and the supporting ill-fated South-East Asia Treaty Organization (SEATO), established in Bangkok in February 1955. The Collective Defence Treaty, or Manila Pact, was a military alliance that initially comprised the US, the UK, France, Australia, New Zealand, Pakistan, Thailand and the Philippines. It was formed as part of the global architecture of containment to hold the line along the seventeenth parallel of latitude in Vietnam against further communist territorial advance. However, the Treaty created dissent from the outset, as well as confusion over its role with reference to the source of military threat. In the event, neither the Manila Pact nor SEATO demonstrated either a viable political purpose or a military function. The Manila Pact's multilateral utility was compromised in March 1962 when a joint statement by then US Secretary of State Dean Rusk and Thai Foreign Minister Thanat Khoman asserted that the Treaty obligations did not depend on the prior agreement of all parties because the obligations were individual as well as collective. The US did not invoke the Collective Defence Treaty to support its military intervention during the Vietnam War. Instead, an alternative *ad hoc* grouping of regional allies was established to provide political support for the intervention. SEATO was officially disbanded in June 1977. The *ad hoc* alliance has survived only nominally, although the United States reaffirmed its commitment to the Manila Pact in February 1979 in support of Thailand following Vietnam's invasion of Cambodia.[6]

In September 1951, a smaller multilateral alliance was created. The ANZUS Treaty – comprising Australia, New Zealand and the United States – reflected the need to reassure the United States' antipodean allies that its policy of rehabilitating Japan to counter communist China would not revive the kind of threat that Japan had posed in the early 1940s. The ANZUS Treaty has never been invoked and was frustrated in its practical purpose of multilateral security cooperation by the anti-nuclear policy of a Labour Party administration in Wellington in the mid-1980s. It has survived primarily as a framework for Australian–US security cooperation.[7]

A UK-inspired multilateral alliance formation was more propitious. The August 1957 Anglo-Malayan Defence Agreement, with which Australia and New Zealand also became associated in 1959, was extended to the newly formed Federation of Malaysia in September 1963 and then modified again when Singapore gained its independence on expulsion from the Federation in August 1965. This Agreement proved its worth as an instrument of collective defence during Indonesia's abortive 'Confrontation' of Malaysia in 1963–66. 'Confrontation' was a form of coercive diplomacy that used military means short of all-out war to create an international crisis in order to provoke diplomatic intervention in Indonesia's favour. When in the late 1960s the UK had to come to terms with its waning power and announced the withdrawal of its military presence east of Suez, the firm commitment of the 1957 Defence Agreement gave way in November 1971 to consultative Five-Power Defence Arrangements with the same membership.

These Five-Power Defence Arrangements have never been invoked, although they do still operate in reduced form with an air-defence system for peninsula Malaysia and annual military exercises. A significant feature of the Arrangements is the way in which defence cooperation between Malaysia and Singapore in particular has served the political function of confidence-building. Malaysia and Singapore have been partners within ASEAN from its creation in 1967. Their relationship has been marred, however, by tension rooted in a racial conflict between Malays and Chinese which led to Singapore's expulsion from the Federation. Such multilateral security arrangements have had a political purpose, justified ostensibly by military provision for external defence.[8]

ASEAN, however, is a very different form of multilateralism to those discussed above, and lacks any formal military dimension. Moreover, it was established by South-east Asian states alone without the intervention or support of a major external power. At the time, ASEAN's founding members – Thailand, Malaysia, Singapore, Indonesia and the Philippines – were united by a shared anti-communist sentiment, and by concern for the outcome of the Vietnam War and its effect on the US commitment to regional security. ASEAN was set up primarily, however, to provide an institutional framework for intra-regional reconciliation and to establish a corresponding trust among former adversaries following Indonesia's practice of Confrontation. This reconciliation also had a security dimension beyond simply ending wars. It would enhance political stability, both nationally and regionally, through the fullest allocation of national resources to economic development. ASEAN's founding members were joined by Brunei in January 1984 and by Vietnam in July 1995. Vietnam's accession, well after the end of the Cold War, was a historic act of reconciliation, although the government in Hanoi has retained its communist identity.

The preamble to ASEAN's founding declaration expresses the aspiration to take a proprietary role in managing regional order. Yet ASEAN initially articulated its declared functions in explicitly non-political terms. The Association's early experience was chequered. It almost foundered in the late 1960s when the Philippines revived its claim to the Malaysian state of Sabah in northern Borneo. Relations between Singapore and Indonesia were also severely tested when the Singapore government insisted in October 1968 on hanging two Indonesian marines found guilty of acts of terror during the period of Confrontation. In February 1976, however, after the dramatic fall of the three Indochinese states to revolutionary communism, the ASEAN heads of government met together for the first time on Bali. The resultant Declaration of ASEAN Concord, registering a corporate political identity and a commitment to regional stability, demonstrated the states' common purpose and collective nerve. The Declaration endorsed an earlier commitment by the ASEAN states in November 1971 to make South-east Asia a Zone of Peace, Freedom and Neutrality (ZOPFAN), 'free from any form or manner of interference by outside powers'.[9] This commitment had been precipitated by the PRC's assumption of China's seat at the United Nations the previous October, and announced to external powers that the ASEAN states reserved the right to define the terms of their own regional order.

At their February 1976 meeting in Bali, the ASEAN heads of government also concluded a Treaty of Amity and Cooperation for South-east Asia which codified norms for managing regional order that had first been set out as guidelines for realising a ZOPFAN by the ASEAN foreign ministers in April 1972.[10] These norms were unexceptional, emphasising respect for national sovereignty, non-interference in another state's domestic affairs and renouncing the threat or use of force in settling disputes. The Treaty of Amity and Cooperation has been described as an example of a 'security through peace approach' which fails to make practical provision for addressing the role of force in conflict and in its resolution.[11] Indeed, defence cooperation was specifically excluded from ASEAN's corporate agenda, although it was sanctioned on an inter-governmental basis outside the Association primarily as a confidence-building measure.

The ASEAN members had by then begun to develop a practice of close consultation and cooperation among their ministers and senior officials. This facilitated both ASEAN's internal and regional roles, and gave rise to a distinctive security culture of conflict avoidance and conflict management, albeit idealised in terms of the corporate interest. The Association's practice of consultation and cooperation has conspicuously avoided formal multilateralism in favour of informal private bilateral arrangements to address particular tensions between member governments. ASEAN's official secretariat of some 20 years' standing in Jakarta, has always been kept in a subordinate position to the foreign ministries of the member governments. Moreover, although the Treaty of Amity and Cooperation made provision to establish formal mechanisms for settling disputes, it has never been invoked for that purpose.

Tan Sri Ghazali Shafi, a former Foreign Minister of Malaysia who, as a senior official, was present at ASEAN's founding Bangkok conference in August 1967, indicated in 1992 the nature of the understanding that ASEAN's member-governments had entered into at the outset. In the mid-1960s, he and an Indonesian counterpart, General Ali Moertopo, had been charged with promoting reconciliation between the then adversaries Malaysia and Indonesia within the framework of wider regional cooperation. They recommended in particular 'that inter-state problems should not be aired openly no matter how small'.[12] Ghazali states: 'We were recommending a special kind of relationship conscious of the fact that the modern state entities in the region were the product of colonial designs which had left a number of thorny residual problems, particularly in relation to national borders'. In working to overcome the mutual hostility created by Indonesia's practice of Confrontation against Malaysia, Ghazali and Moertopo avoided any explicitly Western notions of how to organise groups of states in cooperative security. Instead, they drew on a common cultural heritage in which 'the effective management of political problems should be emphasized. Leaders at all levels and in all sectors should be regularly exposed to each other through personal meetings'.

Yet there would not seem to be anything distinctively South-east Asian, beyond the idiom employed, about such a prescription for promoting mutual trust. It has long been accepted that personal relationships can shape political ones, both positively and negatively. That said, Ghazali and Moertopo's prescription was honoured largely because Indonesia, under the new government of General, later President, Suharto, made it a conscious policy to exchange its erstwhile role of regional troublemaker for that of constructive partner. Suharto was motivated to do so by the serious state of Indonesia's economy, that had fallen victim to former President Sukarno's romantic nationalism. Nonetheless, the fact that the largest, most populous and potentially most powerful state in South-east Asia was prepared to make such a commitment gave ASEAN remarkable political ballast from the very outset.

If ASEAN as a new venture in multilateralism was based on a historical model, it was neither openly declared nor consciously apparent. An obvious analogy, however, would seem to be the Concert of Europe which existed during the early nineteenth century.[13] The Concert of Europe restored France, a failed aspirant hegemon, to the comity of European states in the interest of dynastic legitimacy, to counter domestic revolutionary challenges and to uphold regional order. The Concert of Europe had been predicated on the concept of the balance of power, but in the second half of the twentieth century this notion was anathema to a non-aligned Indonesia whose participation in ASEAN was critical to the Association's existence and viability. Yet without identifying it with European practice, ASEAN was established with balance of power clearly in mind. President Suharto well understood that one way to restore regional confidence and stability would be to lock Indonesia into a structure of multilateral partnership and constraint that would be seen as a rejection of hegemonic pretensions. While France had participated in the Congress of Vienna in 1815 as a defeated and contrite state, Indonesia took part in ASEAN's founding conference in 1967 without any such diplomatic disability. It assumed responsibilities for regional order as the effective *primus inter pares* of the Association. The extent to which Indonesia's example of political self-denial in the interest of regional order may be emulated within the wider Asia-Pacific is central to any parallel between ASEAN and the ASEAN Regional Forum.[14]

An ASEAN Model
Since its creation, ASEAN has comprised a diverse set of states with a variety of bilateral tensions. These tensions have arisen in part from disputes over the territorial legacies of colonialism, reinforced in the

South-east Asian mainland by historical antagonisms that pre-date the colonial experience. Ties within ASEAN have been tested by the allure of separatism and irredentism where the colonial political boundaries of successor states have cut across zones of cultural homogeneity, as well as by conflict over offshore islands valued partly for their access to maritime space and resources under the law of the sea. Malaysia is the extreme example of such bilateral tensions. With two wings – in the Malay peninsula and northern Borneo – Malaysia shares land and/or maritime borders with every other ASEAN state, including Vietnam. Bilateral tensions have been aggravated in some cases by personality clashes between political leaders, most marked in the case of Indonesia and Malaysia.[15]

These bilateral tensions have never been serious enough, so far, to constitute a *casus bellum*. Nonetheless, the ASEAN governments have been determined not to allow such tensions to jeopardise their common goals of state-building and regime maintenance based on economic development. Moreover, a cardinal as well as self-serving principle shared by all ASEAN members is non-interference in each other's domestic affairs. This precept would be severely tested if separatist and irredentist causes were actively pursued across borders.

In addition to coping with these underlying bilateral tensions, ASEAN has been divided over its strategic perspective – specifically, over whether or not it should manage the regional balance or distribution of power on an exclusive basis. This divided outlook persists despite ASEAN's declared commitment to a ZOPFAN. The lack of consensus within ASEAN reflects the different geopolitical circumstances of its member-states, and the concern of some of them that their regional partners are also potential adversaries. The lack of a shared definition of common external threat was clearly evident during the Cambodian conflict. It has also been an obstacle to collective defence arrangements, while any attempt at intra-mural collective security arrangements would almost certainly have created more problems than it would have solved. ASEAN's options in addressing regional security have thus been limited.

Within ASEAN, security has always been addressed through consultation and dialogue rather than through conventional collective security and formal mechanisms for settling disputes. This is the essence of the so-called ASEAN model to which Indonesia made a major conceptual contribution in pioneering and promoting 'national resilience' with security conceived of in non-military terms. This ideal condition would be achieved by creating a stable domestic political order that would encourage fruitful economic development.

In turn, this economic growth would reinforce the underlying political order. The ideal aggregate expression of 'national resilience' in South-east Asia as a whole was seen as 'regional resilience' – a condition in which regional cooperation would reduce external threat and prevent internal political disorder from spreading across common borders. It would also deny extra-regional predators the opportunity to fish in troubled waters, and facilitate economic interest and investment by external partners. Regional resilience would then reinforce both domestic and regional stability. It has been observed that 'if each member nation can accomplish an overall national development and overcome internal threats, regional resilience can result in much the same way as a chain derives its strength from the strength of its constituent parts'.[16]

Addressing security through a presumed synergy between national and regional resilience, repudiating both collective defence and conventional collective security, became ASEAN's operational security doctrine. At the same time, however, individual states could still maintain their security links with extra-regional powers that had been established prior to membership in ASEAN, with the notable exception of Indonesia.

A network of bilateral security cooperation beyond ASEAN has grown over the years, culminating in an unprecedented security agreement between Indonesia and Australia in December 1995. Australia engages in bilateral military cooperation with every ASEAN state, including Vietnam, whose armed forces receive English-language training to enable them to participate in confidence-building operations.[17] Other examples of bilateral defence cooperation beyond ASEAN include a UK battalion of Gurkha Rifles in Brunei whose tenure was renewed in December 1994, the United States' annual *Cobra Gold* military exercises with Thailand, and the continued US commitment to its 1951 mutual security agreement with the Philippines, which it demonstrated with bilateral military exercises in April and May 1996. Singapore provides perhaps the most striking examples of bilateral defence cooperation beyond ASEAN, and has used military training facilities in Australia, Israel, Taiwan and the United States. The US, as indicated above, has entered into limited post-Cold War military access arrangements with Singapore, Malaysia, Indonesia and Brunei.

The fact that such bilateral defence links have been retained and expanded demonstrates the extent to which ASEAN's operational security doctrine has depended on a supporting pattern of power in which the United States has played the critical balancing role.

Uncertainty about future US military deployments and intentions in the Asia-Pacific after the end of the Cold War concentrated ASEAN minds on security in a wider regional context.

Over time, it became clear that ASEAN was not about formal dispute settlement or conflict resolution *per se*, but rather about creating a regional milieu in which such problems either did not arise or could be readily managed and contained. The need for carefully coordinated diplomatic responses to the Cambodian conflict from 1978 enhanced ASEAN's ability to generate a climate of mutual confidence among its partners in which to cope with bilateral tensions. On Cambodia, ASEAN demonstrated its quality of a diplomatic community, able to speak, most of the time, with one voice on matters of regional import. Moreover, the cardinal rule of international society – the sanctity of national sovereignty – violated by Vietnam's invasion, was at the heart of ASEAN's Treaty of Amity and Cooperation. Indeed, it was ASEAN's effective *raison d'être* as a regional organisation.[18]

The Cambodian conflict bestowed on ASEAN a unique regional and international role, albeit underpinned by Cold War diplomatic alignments that masked the Association's limitations. During the conflict, ASEAN's international standing was reinforced by its ability immediately after the annual meeting of its foreign ministers to command the presence of counterparts from the US, Japan and other industrialised investment and trading partners, including the European Community (now the European Union). These Post-Ministerial Conferences (PMC) with so-called dialogue partners, which evolved concurrently with ASEAN itself, together with separate meetings at both ministerial and officials levels, provided an important diplomatic network for the Association. At the same time, ASEAN's diplomatic community aspect was reinforced when it joined its major trading and investment partners within the ASEAN-PMC in collectively managing economic dialogue.[19]

ASEAN Enters a New Security Context

The primary role in resolving the Cambodian conflict was assumed by the permanent members of the United Nations Security Council, thus exposing ASEAN's diplomatic limitations. Correspondingly, the Association viewed the transformation of the regional security context following the end of the Cold War with some trepidation. It faced losing its broader regional role, as well as experiencing renewed vulnerability. This was highlighted by the way in which contending jurisdictions in the South China Sea – especially the Spratly Islands, an extensive group of islets, reefs and atolls with no distinct geographic definition or settled human population – both succeeded Cambodia as the central conflict in South-east Asia, and linked South-east and North-east Asia in a disturbing geopolitical fusion.[20]

Within ASEAN, Brunei, Malaysia and the Philippines had limited, and to some extent overlapping, claims to the Spratly Islands which ASEAN made no attempt to address. Claims to the entire Spratly group had long been made by China (including Taiwan) and Vietnam. Their bilateral relationship had deteriorated steadily from the early 1970s and they saw the Spratly conflict as symptomatic of their deep-seated historical differences. The determination of both states to extend their maritime domains, primarily at the expense of the other, caused anxiety within ASEAN that focused, in particular, on China. ASEAN viewed China with apprehension not only because of its size, population, geographic proximity and its economic and military potential, but also because of its past interventions on behalf of revolutionary movements and its burgeoning commercial links with regional ethnic Chinese communities.

In February 1992, the Standing Committee of China's National People's Conference approved a law on territorial waters and contiguous areas. This law not only reaffirmed China's extensive claims to all the islands in the South China Sea, but also appeared to claim all the interjacent waters following a map drawn in 1947 by the ousted nationalist regime of Chiang Kai Shek. These extensive claims extended China's potential sovereign jurisdiction some one thousand nautical miles to the south of its mainland. If these claims were realised, China would effectively encompass the maritime heart of South-east Asia, with disturbing implications for ASEAN. Because the pattern of regional alignments had changed following the Cold War and the settlement of the Cambodian conflict, ASEAN and China were no longer in tacit alliance confronting Vietnam. Moreover, their one-time complementary interests had turned into underlying conflict as ASEAN's diplomatic role and influence were no longer underpinned by the major powers. US support was no longer as readily available, as its impending departure from its military bases in the Philippines demonstrated, while China's growing military power could well be deployed against the interests of one or more ASEAN states. This apprehension was reinforced in February 1995 when it was revealed that Chinese naval forces had seized the unoccupied Mischief Reef in the Spratly Islands, claimed also by the Philippines, some 130 miles off the coast of the Philippines island of Palawan.

ASEAN's options in response to this challenge were limited. Even if the Association had overcome its institutional reluctance to collective defence arrangements, the combined military capabilities of its member-states would almost certainly have been inadequate to contain China's intrusive presence in the South China Sea. More fundamentally, ASEAN strongly resisted any confrontation with China because of its likely impact on the region's economic activity, let alone its security. Indeed, access to a burgeoning Chinese market and investment opportunities have persistently constrained such an approach to China. The prevailing view within the Association was that any attempt to confront China would introduce an unnecessary and destructive tension into regional relationships. Instead, it was deemed more practical to try to exploit China's self-declared priority interest in economic development and cooperation, and in a peaceful international environment, to persuade it to curb its irredentist aspirations.

Despite this changed environment, the rising tensions over the South China Sea made some ASEAN members keen to register the Association's continuing prerogative role in the region. In reaction to China's announcement of its law on territorial waters in February 1992, and to its grant the following May of an oil exploration concession in the South China Sea to the US Crestone Corporation, ASEAN's foreign ministers, at the initiative of the Philippines, issued a Declaration on the South China Sea at their annual meeting in Manila in July 1992. The Declaration called on claimants to refrain from using force and to settle contending jurisdictions peacefully. To that end it drew attention to ASEAN's Treaty of Amity and Cooperation in South-east Asia. The Declaration was, in fact, the by-product of a series of Indonesian-inspired unofficial workshops on managing potential conflicts in the South China Sea begun in 1990 with Canadian finance.[21] Indonesia, despite its adventure in Confrontation, had never formally pressed irredentist claims on any of its neighbours other than the colonial Dutch in West New Guinea, now Irian Jaya. That contrast with China differentiated the circumstances of ASEAN's formation from the background to the formation of the ARF.

The Declaration on the South China Sea was ASEAN's attempt to maintain its role in shaping regional order, but its diplomatic impact was far less than that registered during the Cambodian conflict. The changed pattern of international and regional alignments had reduced ASEAN's political significance. China's response to the Declaration, which it interpreted as directed against its irredentist interests, was equivocal, even though its Foreign Minister, Qian Qichen, had attended the Manila meeting as a guest of the Association. The United States was similarly unenthusiastic about the Declaration. The US appeared to have distanced itself from the issue of jurisdiction in the South China Sea and had made it clear that its obligations to the Philippines under their 1951 Treaty of Mutual Security did not extend to Filipino-claimed territories in the Spratly Islands. In one sense, the Declaration on the South China Sea could be interpreted as ASEAN recovering its collective diplomatic voice after being marginalised over Cambodia. In another sense, it exemplified ASEAN's diplomatic impotence and demonstrated the need for an additional framework to address regional concerns.

Thus, in a transformed regional security context, ASEAN embarked on a wider venture in multilateralism but based on its own experience and record. In doing so, its members took the calculated risk of prejudicing ASEAN's corporate identity and prerogative place within South-east Asia. Indeed, in looking beyond the Association, ASEAN was forced to revise its declaratory ZOPFAN doctrine, which had been interpreted as a warning sign to external powers to keep out. Although the Association offered its own model of cooperative security as a framework for an extended multilateral structure, its underlying goal was to create the conditions for a stable balance or distribution of power among the three major Asia-Pacific states – China, Japan and the United States – that would benefit regional order. It was a source of acute concern that a US strategic withdrawal from the region, symbolised by its ready abdication of military base rights in the Philippines, as China emerged as a potentially dominant regional power, might cause Japan to review its non-threatening security doctrine with disturbing regional repercussions.

For ASEAN, a constructive regional order would ideally be based on the balancing military engagement of the United States. This would allow Japan to continue its limited security policy which in turn would be critical in encouraging China to conduct its regional relations according to those norms that had served the general interests of the ASEAN states so well. The policy of balance of power was alien, in principle, to ASEAN's security culture. But the primary collective goal was to promote a balance or distribution of power that would enable the Association to maintain its operational security doctrine without provision for collective defence. The Chairman's Statement issued after the first meeting of senior officials from ASEAN and its PMC dialogue partners in Singapore in

May 1993 that paved the way for the ASEAN Regional Forum observed: 'The continuing presence of the United States, as well as stable relationships among the United States, Japan, and China and other states of the region would contribute to regional stability'.[22]

II. EXTENDING ASEAN'S MODEL

In May 1993 in Singapore, the seed was sown for the new venture in multilateral security dialogue for the Asia-Pacific. ASEAN's senior officials had taken the decision to convene such a meeting in Singapore the previous January, which was then endorsed by the Standing Committee. At the time, Singapore chaired the Association's Standing Committee and the meetings of its senior officials. The Committee comprises the foreign minister of the government that will host the forthcoming annual meeting of ASEAN foreign ministers, and the resident heads of the Association's diplomatic missions. The Committee organises the Annual Ministerial Meeting and any other inter-sessional activities, especially meetings of senior officials. At their May 1993 meeting, ASEAN's senior officials (in effect, the permanent secretaries of the respective foreign ministries) were joined for the first time by their counterparts from the ASEAN-PMC dialogue partners.

Until January 1992, the formal process of ASEAN-PMC dialogue had been confined to matters of economic cooperation. It had included, for example, the issue of financial assistance to deal with the influx of refugees from Indochina, although informally discussions went well beyond purely economic matters. The fourth meeting of ASEAN's heads of government held in Singapore in January 1992, presided over by Singapore's Prime Minister Goh Chok Tong, took the landmark decision to address security cooperation openly through 'external dialogue'. It recommended that 'ASEAN should intensify its external dialogues in political and security matters by using the ASEAN Post-Ministerial Conferences'.[1] A multilateral structure that had evolved almost inconspicuously to fulfil one role was thus being called upon to fulfil another very different one to accommodate the striking changes in the regional security context following the end of the Cold War. The summit's mandate was taken forward by ASEAN's foreign ministries the following year.

At the meeting of ASEAN and ASEAN-PMC senior officials in May 1993, Singapore, with strong backing from Australia and the United States, went further and recommended expanding the existing ASEAN-PMC dialogue structure. There was some resistance from Indonesia, Thailand and Japan, which were nervous about moving beyond the familiar context of the Western-aligned ASEAN-PMC. In the event, the meeting recommended the additional membership of China and Russia, with which ASEAN had begun to develop consultative partner relationships in July 1991, and of Vietnam and

Laos, which had been accorded observer status within ASEAN – together with Papua New Guinea, a long-time observer – on acceding to the Association's Treaty of Amity and Cooperation in July 1992. At the conclusion of their meeting, the senior officials agreed 'that there was a window of opportunity for countries in the region to strengthen and promote political and security conditions for economic growth and development'. This accord echoed the spirit and logic of ASEAN's operational security doctrine.

In July 1993, all 18 governments concerned dispatched their foreign ministers to a special meeting in Singapore, convened to coincide with ASEAN's Annual Ministerial Meeting.[2] At a formal dinner, they agreed that a separate gathering of the foreign ministers would be arranged, to be called the ASEAN Regional Forum. This would hold its first working session in Bangkok in July 1994, again close to the date of ASEAN's Annual Ministerial Meeting, and would be chaired by Thailand's Foreign Minister, Prasong Soonsiri, who was also to preside over the ASEAN meeting. Thus began a novel venture in multilateral security dialogue whose declared objective was to develop 'a predictable and constructive pattern of relationships in the Asia-Pacific'. The ASEAN-PMC senior officials' meeting in Singapore in May had reached the same conclusion. While the initiative for the ARF had come from ASEAN, the structure employed was that of the expanded ASEAN-PMC.[3]

The very title of the new entity testified to the Association's regional credentials and diplomatic standing. ASEAN itself had superseded an existing but smaller regional grouping, the Association of South-East Asia (ASA). This grouping had been set up in July 1961 by Malaya (the political core of Malaysia), the Philippines and Thailand, but Indonesia, among other regional states, had refused to participate. ASA was short lived. It was an indirect casualty of Confrontation, which had encouraged the Philippines to press a territorial claim to Sabah at the expense of its relations with Malaya and then Malaysia. Its members had deemed it appropriate after the end of Confrontation in mid-1966 to establish a completely new regional entity to engage Indonesia as a potential regional hegemon in a way that the new and responsible government in Jakarta would not find politically demeaning. This was done at the expense of the ASA, which was allowed to lapse.[4]

In 1993, however, ASEAN was not sacrificed to save the face of Vietnam, another contrite regional troublemaker within South-east Asia. Nor was it sacrificed to accommodate the changes in the Asia-Pacific post-Cold War security context. ASEAN had been too successful a vehicle for confidence-building and preventive diplomacy within South-east Asia, and its member-states had too strong a stake in its institutional continuity to allow it to lapse. Vietnam, perceived as a regional troublemaker because of its Soviet-backed military intervention in Cambodia in 1978, had called for an alternative regional organisation to ASEAN in the mid-1970s. Two decades later, in July 1995, the Vietnamese government was only too pleased to join the Association on ASEAN's terms. In that time, Vietnam had changed from a triumphalist revolutionary state to a diplomatic supplicant as its domestic and regional circumstances declined after its ill-fated Cambodian intervention. Membership in ASEAN was essential if Vietnam was to overcome a disturbing vulnerability, especially in its relations with a hostile China.[5] Yet, without actually sacrificing the Association, the changing global and regional circumstances required a different and wider structure of cooperative relations for managing security problems that would span both South-east and North-east Asia, well beyond the competence of ASEAN alone.

The landmark decision taken at the ASEAN heads of government meeting in January 1992 reflected a growing regional consensus over the merits of expanding the bounds of cooperative security. For example, a corresponding recommendation to that made at the Singapore summit had been proposed the previous June by a number of regional institutes of strategic and international studies, collectively known as ASEAN-ISIS, influenced by advice from a senior official in Japan's Foreign Ministry.[6] Even earlier, in 1990, the foreign ministers of Australia and Canada had separately proposed an Asia-Pacific conference on security and cooperation inspired by the Cold War experience in particular of the Conference for Security and Cooperation in Europe (CSCE). At the ASEAN-PMC in Kuala Lumpur in July 1991, Japan's Foreign Minister, Taro Nakayama, had put forward a similar proposal to that of ASEAN-ISIS, based on the role of the ASEAN-PMC in which he advocated that it should be used to create 'a sense of mutual reassurance'. His terminology was carefully chosen, deliberately excluding the concept of confidence-building, which Tokyo regarded as a process to be entered into only by adversaries.[7]

Despite its external provenance, Nakayama's initiative was received sympathetically by ASEAN's foreign ministers. The US Bush administration, however, was deeply suspicious of any prospective multilateralism in the Asia-Pacific that might undermine the utility and credibility of existing bilateral arrangements to which the

United States was committed. Then US Secretary of State, James Baker, was not prepared to think beyond 'a hub and spokes' model of regional security and his view prevailed. Moreover, before the break-up of the Soviet Union in December 1991, the US was reluctant to give it any opportunity to claim a role in Asia-Pacific security arrangements, as Mikhail Gorbachev had proposed as early as July 1986 in a speech in Vladivostok. Japan's initiative was significant, however, in indicating its sustained and deep reluctance to assume a conventional regional security role and to revise island defence plans for such a wider purpose. A multilateral security dialogue that did not jeopardise Japan's special security relationship with the United States fitted well into its long-standing approach to the region which precluded a forward military role. Underlying Foreign Minister Nakayama's initiative was an attempt to encourage a new structure of regional relations that would perpetuate US military engagement. At the time, it was not intended to include China; nor for that matter the Soviet Union. Japan feared above all that a US military withdrawal from East Asia might spark off a dangerous competition for regional hegemony from which Tokyo would not be able to distance itself.[8]

By January 1992, however, ASEAN was ready to take a critical step in the direction proposed by Nakayama, so overcoming its long-standing reluctance to venture directly and explicitly into regional security matters, especially with major powers outside South-east Asia. ASEAN's willingness to do so beyond the ASEAN-PMC had been set out clearly in the Chairman's Statement issued at the end of the seminal meeting of senior officials in Singapore in May 1993. Moreover, the contribution made by the balance of power to regional security had been accepted implicitly in ASEAN's tentative move towards creating a multilateral security dialogue. The prime role in that undertaking was allocated to the United States, whose regional presence, alongside that of China and Japan, was considered critical to any new security architecture. Indeed, at the time, sustained US military engagement following its withdrawal from Subic Bay naval base took priority over the so-called comprehensive engagement of China. To that end, as cited in Chapter I, the Chairman's Statement maintained:

> The continuing presence of the United States, as well as stable relationships among the United States, Japan, and China, and other states of the region would contribute to regional stability.

Added to the aspiration to stable regional relationships was the belief that an economic nexus and interdependence would underpin and serve its cause: 'The economic underpinnings of security and the need for continued dialogue and firm links with global and regional partners were also stressed'.

In November 1989, at Australia's initiative, a new form of multi-lateral economic structure, the Asia-Pacific Economic Cooperation (APEC), had emerged which has since been sustained in institutional form through a small secretariat based in Singapore.[9] APEC assumed a political significance in November 1993 when, following a proposal by US President Bill Clinton, annual meetings of heads of government (with special arrangements made in the case of Taiwan and Hong Kong) were added to those of its economic ministers. APEC's formation reflected regional concerns about developing restrictive trading blocs outside Asia, as well as the burgeoning sense of self-confidence among Asia-Pacific states that came from their astounding economic achievements which the World Bank was to describe, somewhat less than accurately, as the 'East Asian Miracle'.[10]

The senior officials of ASEAN and its PMC dialogue partners were intent on creating a regional security structure analogous to APEC. The way in which a stable regional environment had contributed to economic growth which, if sustained, would in turn strengthen the foundations of security in a mutually self-reinforcing process gave them added confidence. APEC's corporate experience confirmed ASEAN's belief in the synergy between national and regional resilience, which it was ready to apply to a wider Asia-Pacific in a post-Cold War context.

In formally taking the lead to promote the ARF, the Association's governments had a very clear model in mind regarding its approach to security. They conceived of the ARF as an ASEAN writ large, extending into North-east Asia and the Pacific the understandings and practices that had informed the relatively successful workings of the Association. The ARF's very foundation, however, was also an acknowledgement by the ASEAN governments that they were not competent collectively to deal effectively with post-Cold War regional security problems. In an attempt to cope with those problems, ASEAN had been obliged to expand its strategic horizons. In so doing, it took the calculated risk that the central role ASEAN had assumed, up to a point, within most of South-east Asia might be prejudiced and diminished by the political weight of the major Asia-Pacific powers, which it was deemed imperative to include within the new multilateral structure. APEC's formation in 1989 had also been an important spur to ASEAN's commitment to establish its own free trade area at its fourth summit in January 1992.

In the event, ASEAN had little option but to widen the multilateral dialogue to the rest of the Asia-Pacific because it had become impossible in security terms to conceive of South-east Asia as a separate entity. Underlying this initiative, however, was the shared assumption that the end of the Cold War would provide a breathing space in which a multilateral security dialogue would engage the major Asia-Pacific powers in a structure of stable relationships. After the crisis in the Taiwan Strait in March 1996, it is important to note that the issue of Taiwan's confrontation with China, which revived Sino-US tensions, was never intended to come within the remit of the ARF. A fundamental distinction was drawn between membership in the ARF and membership of APEC, within which China has tolerated Taiwanese participation with an appropriate title intended to undermine its claim to statehood.

ASEAN's Leading Role

ASEAN was able to play a central diplomatic role in promoting and defining the new multilateral structure for two reasons.[11] First, the Association was an acceptable interlocutor to all the major regional powers. Neither the United States nor Japan wished to take the lead in the undertaking, while China would have been most reluctant to join any multilateral venture formally initiated by either power. China's problematic relations with the US and Japan were based in part on the suspicion that they were engaged in a tacit policy of containment at China's expense. Second, the ASEAN model was particularly appropriate for the post-Cold War era in which regional tensions were no longer expressed in a tangible and imminent common threat that called for a countervailing military coalition. To that extent, the undertaking made no unpalatable political or economic demands on potential members. As a US State Department spokesperson pointed out at the time of the July 1993 meeting at which the decision was taken to establish the ARF: 'We are not talking about setting up instant formal security structures. We're talking about dialogue at this point. We're talking about incrementally exploring how you shore up security in this region'.[12]

To the extent that ASEAN had explored and advocated an incremental 'building-block' approach to multilateral security cooperation based on its past success, without demanding a high political price for such cooperation among regional partners, its model could be commended without generating open opposition. The non-ASEAN states within the ASEAN-PMC, however, had conceded the title 'ASEAN Regional Forum' as a transitional measure only, expecting that in time the structure would become known as the Asian Regional Forum, reflecting its true scope and membership. That prospect has become a source of tension within the ARF as ASEAN insists on retaining the central diplomatic role, supported by China which fears that US interests might dominate the enterprise.

In endorsing a new multilateral process of cooperative security, the ASEAN-PMC senior officials' meeting in May 1993 had addressed non-military means only. They discussed preventive diplomacy and conflict management, non-proliferation – both nuclear and non-nuclear – and confidence-building measures. As the Chairman's Statement indicated: 'There was a convergence of views on the need to find means for consultations on regional political and security issues'. Significantly, the meeting explicitly recognised that ASEAN's Treaty of Amity and Cooperation 'could complement the role of the UN by providing a regional framework to foster positive conditions for peace and security, and to provide measures for preventive diplomacy and dispute resolution'. Although some of the terminology, such as the references to preventive diplomacy and confidence-building measures, was not drawn from ASEAN's political lexicon or formal experience, the approach the meeting adopted and recommended to the governments concerned was inherent in ASEAN's security culture. Although ASEAN had been founded without an explicit security agenda beyond the generalisation in the preamble to its founding declaration, its intra-mural role demonstrated its function as a vehicle for confidence-building and preventive diplomacy according to international principles of common and cooperative security.[13]

In facing up to the realities of the new post-Cold War security context, ASEAN sought to exploit its unique advantage by taking the formal political initiative to advocate its own model of multi-lateralism. In the main, the ASEAN governments were pushing at an open door. In addition to the early leads by Canada and Australia, Japan had also pledged its strong support for a new multilateralism. In January 1993, in a speech in Bangkok, then Prime Minister Kiichi Miyazawa had reiterated his government's earlier plea to Asian and Pacific nations to 'develop a long-term vision regarding the future of peace and security for their region'.[14] This had the underlying purpose of ensuring that the United States remained militarily engaged in the region. By this point, the US had become much more sympathetic to the idea of exploring multilateral arrangements for regional security as a supplement, rather than as an alternative, to its long-standing bilateral arrangements. The Bush administration had subscribed to this view before Bill Clinton had won the presidential election in November 1992 and the US had withdrawn from its military bases in the Philippines.[15]

The newly elected Clinton administration was even more encouraging, as became clear in April 1993 when Winston Lord made a policy statement before the Senate Foreign Relations Committee prior to his confirmation as Assistant Secretary of State for Asia-Pacific Affairs. Moreover, Washington was also interested in creating a vehicle that would encourage dialogue between South Korea and Japan in the absence of any suitable bilateral forum. Both Japan and the US were thus happy for ASEAN to take the diplomatic lead in setting up the new multilateral venture. As indicated above, ASEAN's central diplomatic role was also acceptable to China which would have been reluctant to participate in any new regional security arrangement in which the pre-eminent position was occupied by either the United States or Japan.

Ever since the turbulent and bloody events in Tiananmen Square in June 1989, China's relationship with the United States had been acutely problematic. Beijing was concerned that the US had rein-stated a policy of containment, encouraged by its exclusive position as a global superpower, which had been confirmed by its military success in the Gulf War in early 1991. For its part, the Clinton administration was ready to pursue its ideological agenda of enlarging market democracies which Beijing found highly distasteful because it assumed a licence to interfere in China's domestic affairs by seeking to tie economic cooperation to human rights. China responded to ASEAN's initiative in Singapore with mixed feelings. It was conspicuously evident to Beijing that the core of the new multilateral undertaking was the ASEAN-PMC; in effect, a pro-Western constellation of states.

It would also have been only too clear to China that one of the prime purposes of the May 1993 meeting of senior officials had been to address China's new-found regional latitude following the end of the Cold War. However, the meeting did not address that issue in terms of any imminent threat that China's military modernisation might create. Rather, it saw Beijing's declared economic priorities as offering a unique opportunity to induct China into good international practices in a non-challenging way. This would serve China's own declared interests and ward off any evolving threat to the region in the future. In that respect, Singapore's Prime Minister Goh Chok Tong expressed the view that 'Beijing's involvement in regional dialogue on peace and security was important to ensure that economic competition would not result in conflict'.[16] Irrespective of private misgivings, China responded positively by sending Foreign Minister Qian Qichen to participate in the founding dinner of the ARF in July 1993. Qian Qichen stressed his government's peaceful intent and pointed to China's economic development as a stabilising factor in the region.

Whatever its reservations about being drawn into a potentially constraining multilateral structure, China had good, and self-interested, reasons to become a party to the new venture. Beijing wished to allay regional fears about China's future intent so as not to disrupt a fruitful pattern of economic cooperation. It was also keen to support ASEAN in resisting US pressure to tie human-rights issues to such cooperation. Above all, China was reluctant to be excluded from such an extensive assembly of regional states, even if it did harbour the suspicion that such an assembly might be employed to 'gang up' on China. Coincidentally or not, ASEAN's foreign ministers took the decision to admit Vietnam to membership in July 1994, immediately before the inaugural working session of the ARF.

Before addressing the limited experience of the ARF itself, it should be reiterated that ASEAN has been, from the outset, a club of foreign ministers whose agenda and direction has been strongly influenced by their bureaucratic ministries. It was only in December 1995 that the Association's heads of government decided to convene annual informal summits. The ASEAN Regional Forum, as an extension of ASEAN's model of regional security, was also set up as a club of foreign ministers, but in a part of the world in which foreign ministries are regularly by-passed by defence ministries and prime-ministers' departments. That said, the initiative for the ARF demonstrated a consensus within ASEAN, even if enthusiasm for the undertaking in Singapore in May 1993 was not necessarily shared to the same degree in some other regional capitals. Beneath that consensus lay support for ASEAN's leading role in promoting the multilateral enterprise. That role would seem to be historically unique.

Within the Asia-Pacific, there is no other historical example of a group of lesser states assuming such a diplomatic centrality in fostering a multilateral security arrangement that involved all major regional powers. That centrality would also seem to be at odds with the experience of the nineteenth-century Concert of Europe, since the very notion of a concert is based on the role of major powers as defining members. This was very much the original model for the United Nations Security Council in which its permanent members who, unlike the non-permanent members, have the privilege of a veto and assume the prime responsibility. In the case of the ASEAN Regional Forum, which also has a concert-like quality, the lead was taken by lesser states in the absence of natural concert leaders. In that respect, ASEAN's leading role in promoting the ARF is the result not only of an act of corporate political will, but also of the fact that the major Asia-Pacific powers have been incapable of forming a concert arrangement among themselves.[17]

III. THE ASEAN REGIONAL FORUM TAKES SHAPE

The First Working Session
The founding dinner of the ASEAN Regional Forum, held in July 1993, took place around an oblong table, which ironically restricted multilateral conversation. Nonetheless, in the words of the host, Singapore's Foreign Minister Wong Kan Seng, it was 'a unique occasion and a significant milestone in ASEAN's effort to promote dialogue on regional security'.[1] The central issue for the first working session in Bangkok a year later was whether the embryonic ARF would be able to encourage 'a predictable and constructive pattern of relationships' through dialogue alone. More realistically, there was genuine concern about whether the ARF could be sustained beyond a single meeting.

As mentioned above, an ASEAN model *per se* had never been openly articulated in any document issued by the Association. Instead, its operating premises have to be inferred from nearly three decades of regional cooperation, which can best be described as an institutionalised expression of confidence-building and preventive diplomacy, albeit of an unobtrusive kind. ASEAN's working life has been based on the principle – albeit honoured at times in the breach – of not disclosing publicly any internal differences. Although a group of very unequal states, ASEAN has also enthroned the principle of sovereign equality, which translates into reaching agreement by consensus, even if this involves protracted discussion and decision-making. Indeed, ASEAN has accepted the very act of dialogue as the appropriate mode for strengthening intra-mural relationships in the interest of regional stability. This commitment to dialogue has engendered a quasi-familial corporate culture, with the understanding that the larger member-states would not impose their interests at the expense of the smaller ones.

In practice, ASEAN is replete with bilateral tensions, such as those over territorial and maritime jurisdiction. However, such matters, when addressed rather than avoided, have been dealt with on a bilateral basis rather than through ASEAN as a corporate entity. The Association has made a conscious effort to prevent bilateral differences infecting its body politic and cohesion, which has been facilitated by ASEAN's very small scale and by the degree of homogeneity in its outlook. But this changed when Vietnam became a member in July 1995 and when the Association's fifth summit in Bangkok in December 1995, in the presence of the heads of governments of all ten South-east Asian states, made a collective commitment to an ASEAN of ten states by the year 2000.

By contrast, the ASEAN Regional Forum was created on a much grander scale, and, of necessity, required greater heterogeneity of membership from the outset given the very different regional experiences of South-east and North-east Asia. What remains to be seen is the extent to which the ARF's declared security purpose can be based constructively on the informal ASEAN model that has so successfully served the limited needs of its member-states, which, it must be remembered, have not experienced intractable conflict among themselves.

The ASEAN Regional Forum, however, did not exactly snap into action. Its first working session was only convened in July 1994 in Bangkok, a year after its founding dinner, and virtually at the same time as ASEAN's Annual Ministerial Meeting. At a meeting of senior officials in the Thai capital in May 1994, Australia, with Canadian support, took the initiative for promoting practical confidence-building measures through working groups of officials, similar to those of the CSCE. China's representative, however, resisted, making explicit his government's opposition to any time-table for implementing concrete measures for security cooperation. This clearly reflected China's underlying fear of being drawn into a constricting diplomatic trap. China also expressed concern at the very idea of a chairman's concluding statement out of a corresponding fear of being subject to the discipline of a consensus within a primarily ASEAN-PMC political context.

The first working session of the ARF in July 1994 took place in a drawing room in a suite in the Shangri-La Hotel with the respective foreign ministers deployed alphabetically by country in armchairs, with a senior official seated behind, around a set of small tables arranged in oblong formation. There was disappointment that the United States was being represented by its Deputy Secretary of State, Strobe Talbott, and not by Warren Christopher, who had been kept in Washington by the higher priority of the Middle East peace process. The working session had no agenda, only the single topic of 'Asia-Pacific Security-Challenges and Opportunity', perhaps more appropriate for an academic seminar. In addition, only three hours were allocated for discussion among the 18 foreign ministers which, on an equal basis, permitted each principal participant only ten minutes to address the meeting. Such a measured start was deliberate, however. The unanimous view within ASEAN was that the ARF could only ultimately evolve into an effective mechanism for providing security if and when the member governments felt 'comfortable' with the medium and practice. This was especially true for China which had never participated officially in any form of multilateralism with security in mind beyond the United Nations. The session agreed to encourage a form and process of political socialisation that would promote a greater sense of mutual confidence and trust among its various member governments.

The first working session of the ARF was in part a rhetorical occasion. The discussion, which lacked focus and was certainly not a dialogue, centred on identifying appropriate measures for the ARF's declared purpose, as well as on the pace at which it should proceed. The new entity represented both continuity with and change from ASEAN's experience and practice. The Association's proprietary role was clearly registered in the statement of the Chairman, Thai Foreign Minister Prasong Soonsiri. He began by pointing out that the first meeting of the ARF had been held 'in accordance with the 1992 Singapore Declaration of the Fourth ASEAN Summit, whereby the ASEAN Heads of State and Government proclaimed their intent to intensify ASEAN's external dialogues in political and security matters as a means of building cooperative ties in the Asia-Pacific region'.[2] Apart from describing the meeting as historic, signifying 'the opening of a new chapter of peace, stability and cooperation for Southeast Asia [sic]', and claiming that there had been 'a productive exchange of views on the current political and security situation in the Asia-Pacific region', the Chairman's Statement more or less repeated the aspirations expressed at the earlier formative meetings in Singapore. While this was a clear continuation of ASEAN practice, it also represented a break from it in identifying cooperative security practices that had never been formally articulated or indeed engaged in by the Association. Thus, in addition to the 'productive exchange of views' that enabled the member governments 'to foster the habit of constructive dialogue and consultation on political and security issues of common interest and concern', the ARF would be 'in a position to make significant contributions to efforts towards confidence-building and preventive diplomacy in the Asia-Pacific region'.

ASEAN had never ventured formally into the realm of confidence-building, which had been very much a recent European experience, although bilateral military exercises beyond the confines of the Association had partly been undertaken for such a purpose. Indonesia, uniquely, had contributed to preventive diplomacy by holding informal regional workshops on the South China Sea, outside the ASEAN structure and as a non-claimant state. Canada and Australia, as middle powers, had shown a keen interest in institutionalising confidence-building and had sought to force the pace of the ARF against the wishes of the ASEAN states. They preferred a more gradualist approach based, initially at least, on a loose consultative arrangement. This view corresponded closely with that of China, which pointedly endorsed the consensual approach to discussing regional issues and which had resisted inter-sessional meetings held exclusively among government officials. Nonetheless, Australia was requested to submit a detailed set of prescriptions for security cooperation in Asia-Pacific.[3] Other such submissions from Canada, South Korea and Japan have not entered the public domain.

The formal provision made for confidence-building measures in the ARF indicated that the ASEAN states had found it politic to move with the times beyond their own limited experience of security cooperation. The Chairman's Statement only referred to confidence-building and preventive diplomacy in general terms, however. Ironically, in the absence of a representative from North Korea – which had unsuccessfully sought access to the meeting through its ambassador in Bangkok – the only specific security issues mentioned were the related ones of nuclear non-proliferation and the Korean peninsula. Within the closed session, the issues of Cambodia and the South China Sea were also addressed, but the latter only very briefly. China only just tolerated this discussion, having earlier ruled out any negotiations on the matter within the ARF. China's spokesman had suggested that negotiations over disputed claims in the South China Sea could be pursued bilaterally on the periphery of the meeting, but that his government was not willing to discuss the matter of sovereignty. This issue of real contention, however, was not allowed to mar the ARF's first working session which was primarily concerned with launching the multilateral undertaking. A working dinner after the substantive meeting was, however, critical in reaching effective agreement on how to proceed with the ARF.

The first working session took the major decision to convene the ASEAN Regional Forum on an annual basis. The next meeting was scheduled to be held in Brunei in 1995, again following ASEAN's Annual Ministerial Meeting, with Brunei's Foreign Minister Prince Mohamed Bolkiah in the chair. This proximity to the ASEAN annual meeting again affirmed the Association's diplomatic centrality within the ARF. Brunei's Foreign Ministry was charged, in consultation with the other participants, with advancing the ARF process through collating and studying all the papers and ideas raised during the earlier meeting of ARF senior officials (ARF-SOM) and the ARF working session itself. These would then be submitted to the second ARF in Brunei via a second ARF-SOM. In addition to the initial reference to the mandate accorded by the ASEAN heads of government meeting in Singapore in January 1992, ASEAN's prerogative role was registered by the ARF's agreement to endorse the aims and principles of the Association's Treaty of Amity and Cooperation 'as a code of conduct governing relations between states and a unique diplomatic instrument for regional confidence-building, preventive diplomacy, and political and security cooperation'. That endorsement was more symbolic than practical. The so-called code contained within the Treaty was not in itself a distinctive expression of the culture of intra-ASEAN relationships; it did no more than set out unexceptional norms of state practice, which all members of the United Nations had agreed to on signing the UN Charter.

ASEAN had never formally employed the Treaty in an intra-mural context. Indeed, the Treaty's provision for settling disputes directly contradicted ASEAN's underlying unofficial principle of not bringing bilateral differences into the open for fear of damaging its formal structure. ASEAN had used the Treaty for proprietorial reasons to register its central role in the ARF, a role that had not been so readily conceded by some of the other participants to the ARF process, such as Australia and South Korea. In seeking to enthrone the Treaty as a working document of the Forum, a tension was created between ASEAN's exclusive, albeit declaratory, security doctrine within South-east Asia, and the need to widen the structure of security dialogue within the Asia-Pacific. It would have been logical to have allowed all members of the ARF to accede to the Treaty of Amity and Cooperation. Apart from the reservations of countries such as China, which was then apprehensive over the commitment involved, Indonesia, in particular among ASEAN states, was reluctant for one of the Association's diplomatic possessions to be shared in a way that might blur the boundaries between North-east and South-east Asia and thus dilute the Association's claim to an exclusive managerial regional role. For this reason, ASEAN subsequently attempted to differentiate the mode of adherence to the Treaty between South-east Asian and other member-states, although a precedent had already been set in December 1987 when the Treaty was amended to allow Papua New Guinea's accession.

This episode highlighted the problems ASEAN faced in extending its model of regional security in circumstances where it had no real choice because of the transformation of the security context fusing South-east and North-east Asia. Indeed, it also highlighted the degree to which the very category of South-east Asia had been called into question by the end of the Cold War. In his opening statement at the

July 1994 ASEAN Ministerial Meeting in Bangkok that preceded the ARF's first working session, Singapore's Foreign Minister Shanmugam Jayakumar articulated the rationale for the wider venture in multilateralism, as well as how the ARF should function based on the prior experience of ASEAN. He explained: 'There is no viable alternative to this [the ARF] if we are to sustain the favourable conditions which have taken us years to cultivate. While ASEAN can continue to play an instrumental role in forging predictability, it cannot do so alone for long'.[4]

Jayakumar went on to argue against forcing the pace of the ARF's development on the grounds that such action 'would cause discomfort to some participants and discomfort often means diminished participation'. He clearly had China in mind. Jayakumar's recommended alternative was a step-by-step approach modelled on ASEAN's experience. To that end:

> The ARF has to go through a series of regular meetings committed to free and frank exchanges before graduating to more substantive undertakings. Such has been the history of ASEAN itself, which has through the years developed a level of comfort conducive to a free exchange of views.

Jayakumar reiterated that 'the process whereby ASEAN has developed gives valuable lessons for us when we steer [*sic*] the ARF in subsequent years'. He also expressed the hope that the ARF would take on a life of its own 'at a pace comfortable to all'. This opening statement reflected a consensual view, including the assumption that ASEAN would continue to 'steer' the ARF; an assumption made pointedly by Thailand's Deputy Foreign Minister, Surin Pitsuwan, who maintained that 'ASEAN will always have the driver's seat'.[5]

The first working session of the ASEAN Regional Forum was successful in that it took place without disruptive diplomatic incident and ended with a willingness on the part of the participating governments to meet again a year later.[6] To that extent, the session marked a small but constructive step along a path without clear signposts. Importantly, it also established an agenda which took matters beyond an annual meeting of foreign ministers.

By contrast with ASEAN, which had by then established an encompassing network of well over two hundred meetings a year among different groups and levels of ministers and officials, as well as regular personal visits to the member-states by politicians and senior military officers, the ARF had to construct its own inter-sessional agenda from scratch to create a tangible internal dimension to the new structure of relations. To that end, and after China's resistance to meetings involving government officials had been overcome through the strident intervention of Australia's then Foreign Minister, Gareth Evans, three embryonic initiatives were undertaken: a seminar on building confidence and trust was held in Canberra in November 1994; a seminar on peacekeeping was held in Bandar Seri Begawan in March 1995; and a seminar on preventive diplomacy took place in Seoul in May 1995. The composition of these seminars, involving both officials and academics as well as members of regional think-tanks, was a compromise that took into account China's sensibilities. Reports of these seminars were conveyed to the second working session of the ARF which convened in Brunei in August 1995. At that point in its existence, those initial inter-sessional events were matters of form rather than of substance and the distance which the ARF had yet to travel in influencing the climate of regional relations and individual state behaviour was highlighted by China's seizure of the uninhabited Mischief Reef in the Spratly Islands. This crisis had very clear implications for the new Forum.[7]

At the first working session of the ARF in 1994, China's Foreign Minister Qian Qichen had indicated his government's unease that the issue of contending jurisdictions in the Spratly Islands was being discussed within a multilateral format. He reiterated China's peaceful intentions and ruled out the use or threat of force in settling the dispute, as well as re-stating that his country's priority in regional relations was governed by its plans for economic development. In February 1995, however, Filipino fishermen revealed that Chinese naval forces had seized Mischief Reef, located some 130 miles to the south-west of the island of Palawan, and had constructed block-houses that were flying the PRC flag on top of steel scaffolding. These structures had clearly taken some time to build. Indeed, one Philippines cabinet minister ventured the private opinion that China's initial seizure of the reef had most probably taken place some six months before its established presence had been discovered. If that calculation is even near correct, then the decision to invade the reef could have taken place at around the time, or even before, the first working session of the ASEAN Regional Forum had convened. Moreover, informed sources share the view that the decision to seize the Reef could only have been made at the highest level of China's ruling Communist Party.

This incident brought China into direct diplomatic confrontation for the first time with an ASEAN state over any of the Spratly Islands, and called into question China's intentions in the region despite its declared position. Moreover, it also called into question China's *bona fides* as a member of the ARF, as well as the Forum's ability to persuade its members to conduct themselves according to common norms of self-restraint. For its part, China had grossly miscalculated the likely reactions of the ASEAN states to its naval initiative. Their response indicated both the advantages and disadvantages of engaging China within a multilateral framework of relationships.

ASEAN's initial corporate response to the revelation of China's act of assertiveness was a deafening silence, indicative of internal dissent over how to cope with China as a rising power. In the meantime, intra-ASEAN relations were damaged by a public row between the Philippines and Singapore over Singapore's hanging in March 1995 of a Filipina maid found guilty of murder by a Singapore court. A meeting of ASEAN senior officials, coincidentally also held in Singapore in March 1995, to discuss plans for an inaugural Asia–Europe summit conference in Bangkok the following year proved an opportune occasion for the Association to reaffirm its commitment to its Declaration on the South China Sea which had called on claimant states, with China very much in mind, to resolve their differences over jurisdiction peacefully. This was followed by a pre-planned security dialogue at senior officials level between ASEAN and China which convened in Hangzhou in April. On the eve of this meeting, informally over dinner, the ASEAN delegation closed ranks and demonstrated its solidarity over the South China Sea issue. This display of corporate unity is believed to have caused some surprise and even consternation within China's Ministry of Foreign Affairs. This had some beneficial effect when the second working session of the ARF convened at the beginning of August. The Hangzhou security dialogue was also significant in providing the opportunity for the ASEAN delegation to explain the Association's role and intentions as well as its corporate interest in promoting the ARF. Although somewhat startled by the private diplomatic response to the Mischief Reef episode, the meeting did much to allay any abiding Chinese concerns about the risks of engaging in the ARF process.

The Second Working Session
In addition to the political reverberations over Mischief Reef, the second working session of the ARF took place against some crisis in relations between China and both the US and Japan. China's dispute with the United States was the more serious, and centred on the private visit in June 1995 by Lee Teng Hui, the President of Taiwan,

to Cornell University to receive an honorary degree, despite prior assurances from the US State Department to Beijing that a visa would not be granted. This visit was seen in China as evidence that the US was seeking to renege on commitments implicit in the February 1972 Shanghai Communiqué and in two subsequent joint communiqués, as well as in their January 1979 agreement to establish diplomatic relations. Accordingly, Beijing reacted with fury at what it perceived as a US challenge to China's national sovereignty. In addition to a virulent diplomatic barrage, China took coercive measures by test-firing missiles in the Taiwan Strait, which it repeated, along with military exercises, during the run-up to the Taiwanese presidential elections in March 1996.

As for China's relations with Japan, the sense of grievance was on the Japanese side when China began underground nuclear tests shortly after the nuclear test-ban treaty had been indefinitely extended in May 1995. China was also in difficulty with ASEAN over the South China Sea disputes which led to contention over the preliminary draft of the Chairman's Statement during a meeting of ARF senior officials in Brunei also in May 1995. At that early stage in the ARF's existence its members had a common interest in not alienating China, and a concession was made in agreeing not to raise the issue of the Spratly Islands collectively. Nonetheless, China's Foreign Minister must have been conscious of his country's diplomatic isolation as the working session convened, and this almost certainly had a bearing on the posture he adopted at the meeting. Related to this was Vietnam's admission to the Association at the ASEAN Annual Ministerial Meeting in July 1995, shortly after Washington and Hanoi had established diplomatic relations. The timing of this resumption of relations was almost certainly governed by Vietnam's impending membership of ASEAN. The previous February, Cambodia had acceded to the Treaty of Amity and Cooperation, and was also accorded both observer status within ASEAN and membership of the ARF. Myanmar also acceded to the Treaty, but was not immediately granted either observer status within ASEAN or membership of the ARF.

The second working session of the ARF convened on 1 August 1995 at the home of Brunei's Foreign Minister, Prince Mohamed Bolkiah. It consisted of two two-hour sessions and a short meeting of ministers before dinner. The session was guided by a novel 'Concept Paper' which, although approved in advance through consultation, had effectively been drafted in Singapore's Ministry of Foreign Affairs.[8] The Concept Paper sought to set the tone and pace for the

ARF's development and marked a shift away from the declared informality which had been the hallmark of the ASEAN process. It reflected the ASEAN governments' determination to play a defining role in setting the agenda for the ARF. The Paper identified norms by which the ARF would function, as well as outlining its evolution in three stages: from initial confidence-building, through preventive diplomacy, to ultimate conflict-resolution mechanisms. The notion of mechanisms, however, was later excluded from the Chairman's Statement at China's insistence. The Concept Paper stressed the need for a gradual, evolutionary approach to managing security and recommended two complementary approaches.

The first drew explicitly on ASEAN's modalities and experience in reducing tensions and promoting regional cooperation through informal processes 'without the implementation of explicit confidence-building measures'. It directed attention to well-established practices of consultation and consensus (known in Malay-Indonesian as *Musyawarah-Mufakat*), enhanced by regular high-level visits among ASEAN countries. It was claimed that 'this pattern of regular visits has effectively developed into a preventive diplomacy channel'.

The second approach was based on implementing concrete confidence-building measures which drew on the studies formally undertaken by Brunei since the first ARF working session in 1994. Two lists of proposals were identified: measures that could be explored and implemented by ARF participants in the immediate future; and those that could be explored over the medium and long term, best addressed by non-governmental groups such as ASEAN-ISIS linked to the academic-driven Council for Security Cooperation in Asia Pacific (CSCAP). CSCAP had been established in June 1993 as the culmination of a proliferation of regional security seminars and conferences that began in the late 1980s.[9] These two sets of groups were known respectively and colloquially as 'track one' and 'track two'.

The Concept Paper asserted ASEAN's pivotal and proprietorial role in the ARF within which it had 'undertaken the obligation to be the primary driving force'. This was qualified by the acknowledgement that a successful ARF required 'the active participation of all participants to whose interests and concerns ASEAN should always be sensitive'. The Paper stipulated, however, that the ARF's rules of procedure should be based 'on ASEAN norms and practices and that decisions should be made by consensus and without voting after careful and extensive consultations'. It rejected the idea of a secretariat, maintaining that 'ASEAN shall be the repository of all ARF documents and information and provide the necessary support to sustain ARF activities through the chair of its Standing Committee'. Finally, it was recommended that 'the ARF should also progress at a pace comfortable to all participants'. The term 'participants' was used advisedly to distinguish it from the status of membership associated with ASEAN. In preparing the Concept Paper, attention had been given to the experience of the CSCE and Western academic writings on alternative forms of security cooperation to military arrangements. However, a deliberate attempt had been made to avoid using terms that had arisen and been employed in a Cold War context. The key notion the Paper introduced was that of 'comfortable', whose equivalent in both Chinese and Indonesian is being at ease. This also echoes ASEAN's security culture.

The Concept Paper's attempt to stamp ASEAN's proprietary hallmark on the ARF produced some resistance from other participants, and the Paper was not formally endorsed in the Chairman's Statement. Instead, a number of proposals were adopted 'in the context of the Concept Paper'.[10] While the reference to ASEAN undertaking 'the obligation to be the primary driving force' was reiterated, it was preceded, and not followed as in the Concept Paper, by the recognition that a successful ARF required 'the active, full and equal participation and cooperation of all participants'. There were evident indications that countries which felt their own regional agendas were being neglected resented ASEAN's diplomatic assertiveness and proprietary role within the ARF. South Korea, for example, was irritated by its inability to promote formally its own priority of a North-east Asian dialogue. A heated exchange had taken place at the prior meeting of senior officials in May 1995 at which the permanent secretary of a non-ASEAN foreign ministry had claimed that his non-ASEAN counterparts were being treated as second-class citizens. The major Asian powers, however, and especially China, were not sufficiently troubled by ASEAN's assertion of diplomatic centrality in the ARF to take issue with it, although the US and Japan privately held the view that such centrality should be transitional. Moreover, the challenge to ASEAN's role encouraged China's participation in the ARF. During the course of the second working session, Qian Qichen indicated the strong convergence between ASEAN governments and Beijing over the pace at which the ARF should proceed.[11]

Despite some tension over ASEAN's arrogation of its role as the 'primary driving force', the meeting adopted the substance of the

Concept Paper's recommendations. It identified an essentially consultative security function for the ARF, defined in comprehensive terms beyond solely military aspects, while making clear that the ARF would not be used to impose solutions on participants. To that end, the language of the Concept Paper was employed in stating that 'the ARF process shall move at a pace comfortable to all participants'. Correspondingly, the collective approach to security would be 'evolutionary, taking place in three broad stages, namely the promotion of confidence building, development of preventive diplomacy and elaboration of approaches to conflicts', as opposed to the development of a conflict-resolution mechanism, with the pointed iteration that 'the ARF process is now at Stage 1.'

Annex A of the Concept Paper, which dealt with confidence-building measures, became the basis for future activities when it was agreed to set up two structures to help the Chairman of the ARF-SOM make recommendations to the Forum on implementing its proposals. This cautious approach was expressed in an Inter-Sessional Support Group (ISG) on Confidence Building set up to address, in particular, a dialogue on security perceptions and defence policy papers. In addition, Inter-Sessional Meetings (ISM) were established to deal with cooperative activities, including peacekeeping and search-and-rescue coordination. The difference in name between two identical entities was again an attempt to accommodate Chinese objections, in this case to any impression of continuous institutionalised activities. For this reason, the notion of an inter-sessional support group was used to give the formal impression that it would only function on an *ad hoc* basis.

In the arrangements for inter-sessional activities, the exclusive, central role of ASEAN was modified so that one of its representatives would share the chair with a non-ASEAN counterpart. To that end, it was agreed that Indonesia and Japan would co-chair the ISG on confidence-building measures; Malaysia and Canada would co-chair one ISM on peacekeeping operations; while Singapore and the United States would co-chair the other ISM on search-and-rescue coordination and cooperation. Significantly, China was the only major Asia-Pacific power not to co-chair one of the sessions at that time. The other measures agreed encouraged dialogue and confidence-building through participation in the UN Register of Conventional Arms, but also included the equivocal undertaking that ARF countries would submit either to the Forum or to the ARF-SOM, on a voluntary basis, an annual statement of their defence policies. On pressing matters of regional security, the meeting called for an immediate end to nuclear testing, a resumption of dialogue between North and South Korea, and expressed concern over overlapping sovereignty claims in the region. In conclusion, the foreign ministers expressed the view that their endorsement of specific ideas and proposals had 'provided sufficient direction for the ARF process at this stage'.

The Brunei meeting had coincidentally provided a useful informal opportunity for the Chinese and US Foreign Ministers to defuse the immediate tension between their two countries. This had the inadvertent effect of attracting more press coverage than the ARF session itself. The US Secretary of State's interest in the multilateral enterprise increased significantly after that meeting. The meeting also served one of the ARF's founding aims, which was to secure regular Chinese participation. Indeed, to the extent that ASEAN had been able to impose its own norms and operating procedures on the dialogue process, China had indicated that it was comfortable with the multilateral enterprise on which it had been able to apply a diplomatic brake to its own advantage. In this context, by way of concession to ASEAN in particular, China had associated itself with the Chairman's Statement which referred to a collective concern over competing claims to sovereignty.

That part of the Statement also encouraged all claimants to reaffirm their commitment to the principles contained in relevant international laws and conventions, and also to ASEAN's 1992 Declaration on the South China Sea which had called on them to use peaceful means only in resolving their disputes. The Chinese also went out of their way to acknowledge their recognition of international law, including the United Nations Convention on the Law of the Sea (UNCLOS), as a basis for negotiating a settlement of the Spratly Islands issue. This initiative was greeted as a welcome clarification of their legal position, even though Beijing had not then ratified UNCLOS. China also indicated its willingness to discuss the contentious Spratlys issue with all ASEAN members, marking a move away from the rigid bilateralism on which its representatives had previously insisted.

China's concession was, in fact, one of form only. It showed no willingness whatsoever actually to address competing claims to sovereign jurisdiction, and China consistently reiterated its irrefutable and indisputable rights in the South China Sea. However, given China's acute concern that the US was engaged in a new practice of containment by seeking to renege on its long-standing recognition of a single China, the government in Beijing almost certainly deemed it politic to assuage ASEAN's anxieties up to a point. It was probably for this reason that the leaders of the Association pronounced themselves satisfied with the progress of the ARF, besides being content with the tone of the personal relationships struck among the 19 assembled foreign ministers.

The second working session of the ARF did not differ fundamentally in form from the first. Its tone, however, represented an advance because the participants seemed more at ease with one another and shared a consensus of a kind over what steps to take next, which was reflected in the discussion. Accordingly, the prior agreements over procedures and modalities between their senior officials were ratified, in the main. The meeting was notable also for the presence of defence ministry officials. Their participation in the ARF's inter-sessional activities acknowledged that confidence-building could only proceed effectively with the involvement of defence personnel. The meeting's principal accomplishment was the agreement on norms and procedures that gave the ARF an institutional, if embryonic, identity.

IV. THE UTILITY OF THE ASEAN MODEL

The ARF's future activities, established by the Chairman's Statement, involved two complementary approaches. The first, drawn from ASEAN practice, owed much to the small scale of the South-east Asian enterprise and to its quasi-familial culture of consultation and cooperation. Such informal confidence-building and preventive diplomacy could not be readily transposed to a structure of regional dialogue that encompassed 19 states, with others queuing up to join – including France and the UK, dissatisfied with collective representation in the Asia-Pacific through the European Union. Moreover, the South-east and North-east Asian participants had little experience of, or familiarity with, one another's problems. The latter resented ASEAN's diplomatic centrality in the ARF, concerned that the lack of equal participation would prevent them from addressing their own regional interests fully. These states' frustration with the extent to which the ARF has failed to cater directly for North-east Asian security has created structural tension within the multilateral enterprise.

The practice of conflict avoidance and conflict management, which had become a distinguishing feature of the ASEAN model, was not readily transferable, however, to all conflicts in the Asia-Pacific. The one possible exception was that over sovereignty in the South China Sea, as demonstrated by Beijing's apparent decision not to pose any further physical challenge to the revised status quo, at least for the time being. The issue of Taiwan was excluded from the ARF's scope, as effectively was that of the Korean peninsula in the absence of representation from the North Korean government in Pyongyang. Moreover, the ARF has not set out to emulate ASEAN beyond the manner in which it conducts its annual meetings, which have all lasted less than a day. Meetings at heads of government level, as in both ASEAN and APEC, have not been discussed and are only likely if the ARF were to change its name to the Asia-Pacific Regional Forum. Thus, the ASEAN model has contributed to the ARF in terms of form and, minimally, of substance. In between its annual sessions, the ARF functions through a small number of inter-sessional activities, which in the first instance have only a confidence-building remit, leaving issues of actual conflict untouched in any direct sense. This represents both the strengths and the weaknesses of the ASEAN model. The strengths rest on the culture of constraint that comes from a collective commitment to dialogue, while the weaknesses rest on placing the institution's viability before addressing the practical problems of regional security.

The ARF's inter-sessional activities were intended to serve the same function as ASEAN's informal processes. In January 1996 in Tokyo, the Inter-Sessional Support Group on Confidence-Building identified defence exchanges and defence transparency as issues to be explored further at a second meeting in Jakarta in mid-April. The April meeting recommended limited measures to advance those ends, but failed to make any progress on listings in the UN Register of Conventional Arms or a regional equivalent. The meeting's greatest accomplishment, however, in the light of ASEAN's barely hidden agenda of engaging China, was China's expressed willingness to co-chair with the Philippines the next annual ISG dialogue on confidence-building measures. Will such limited and intermittent dialogue, without fulfilling the milieu-creating role accomplished up to a point by ASEAN within its limited geographic bounds, constitute more than a mere exercise in diplomatic form? An answer of a kind was provided in March 1996 when the Inter-Sessional Meeting on Search and Rescue convened in Hawaii just as China's military intimidation in the Taiwan Strait, intended to influence the political process in Taiwan, escalated. The United States responded not with comprehensive engagement and political dialogue, but by dispatching two carrier battle groups to the area. The ISM on Peacekeeping, which convened in Kuala Lumpur in April 1996, confined itself to discussing the UN's post-Cold War experience, but drew no specific lessons for regional application before adjourning *sine die*. The ISM on Peacekeeping was rekindled, however, at the senior officials' meeting the following month. The ARF's inter-sessional agenda is likely to remain limited in the near future to confidence-building and search-and-rescue cooperation, as well, perhaps, as disaster relief (involving Thailand and New Zealand). Discussion of preventive diplomacy and non-proliferation will be confined to the track-two level.

Ironically, the problems created by the ARF's extensive scale and the variety of conflicts experienced by its sub-regional sectors had to be addressed by ASEAN itself, which is seeking to expand its membership, partly with its role within the ARF in mind. When Vietnam joined ASEAN in July 1995, its Prime Minister, Vo Van Kiet, was eligible to attend the fifth meeting of the Association's heads of government in Bangkok the following December. The December 1995 meeting was notable also for the invited presence of the heads of government of Laos, Cambodia and Myanmar. This was the first time that all ten South-east Asian states had been represented together at that level, and in that respect the meeting was a historic turning-point.

The initial drive for a prospective ASEAN of ten members came from Thailand, which saw in such an expansion an opportunity to register its own centrality within the Association. All prospective members would come from the South-east Asian mainland within which Thailand regards itself, somewhat ambitiously, as the economic hub. Early resistance to Thailand's proposal was overcome when ASEAN took the central role within the ARF, as well as by a new-found enthusiasm for ASEAN's expansion to be complete by the millennium. That goal was readily accepted in Bangkok in December 1995. Laos and Cambodia are due to enter the Association in mid-1997, but some doubt remains over Myanmar, which had not then been accorded observer status, despite its accession to ASEAN's Treaty of Amity and Cooperation in July 1995. In June 1996, Myanmar indicated its wish to join ASEAN in 1998.

Apart from the attraction of realising the aspiration expressed in ASEAN's founding declaration, expanding the Association was also expected to reinforce its diplomatic centrality within the ARF. That centrality was somewhat incongruous given the dominant pattern of power in the Asia-Pacific among China, the United States and Japan. ASEAN's assertion in the ARF Concept Paper that it had a pivotal role to play in the Forum and that it had the obligation to be the primary driving force within it met with some resistance. ASEAN's pivotal role in the ARF had been accepted, however, when it was agreed that the Forum's annual meetings would follow on from those of ASEAN's foreign ministers. ARF's annual meetings would, therefore, be held in the country that was chairing ASEAN's Standing Committee, with its foreign minister presiding over the ARF meeting. ASEAN's ability to retain its pivotal position should the other ARF participants become very frustrated at ASEAN's pace of doing business, with exercises in confidence-building serving as little more than 'getting-to-know-you' occasions, however valuable they might be, was a key question. To that extent, ASEAN faced the daunting task in its agenda-setting and directional role of generating an activism within the ARF that would lend greater substance to its corporate existence.

One way in which ASEAN could retain its so-called pivotal position in the ARF would be through its expansion. An ASEAN of ten members able to demonstrate renewed cohesion and to speak with a single voice might enjoy greater influence within the wider Asia-

Pacific enterprise to ASEAN's corporate advantage. This assumption was fraught with difficulty, however, because of the potential problems of reconciling a process of 'widening' with that of 'deepening'; namely, infusing new and disparate members with the level of quasi-familial spirit that ASEAN had developed when its membership had been confined to no more than six states with relatively similar outlooks. Widening to ten members opened up the prospect of further diversity and intra-mural tensions dissipating ASEAN's corporate energies and testing its cohesion and credibility, as well as its standing within the ARF.

As the putative primary driving force of the Forum, ASEAN faces a structural difficulty. There is an evident paradox in the Association seeking to retain its diplomatic centrality within the ARF. ASEAN has sought to locate the ARF's political centre of gravity within South-east Asia. With the exception of the South China Sea disputes, however, the critical conflicts in the Asia-Pacific are in North-east Asia, and two parties to those conflicts – Taiwan and North Korea – are not represented within the ARF. Taiwan was excluded from the ARF, although it was included in APEC, to ensure China's participation in the Forum. North Korea was not represented because some believed that its participation should be a reward for conducting better relations with South Korea. Although set up on informal, track-two terms, a separate North-east Asian security dialogue, involving the United States, China, Japan and South Korea, has convened on a regular basis, while North Korea's nuclear potential has been addressed directly by the United States. North Korea, however, has not indicated an interest in participating in the separate North-east Asian security dialogue.

An additional paradox arose when the ASEAN heads of government meeting in December 1995 invited India to become a full dialogue partner and, therefore, a participant in the ASEAN-PMC. Membership is a defining issue in any multilateral undertaking because it influences the content of agendas. Although it was justified as a counter-balance to China's regional influence, according India dialogue status raised the complicating prospect of its membership of the ARF. This could draw the complex disputes of South Asia into the ARF's ambit, together with an attendant demand from Pakistan for its equal participation. Indonesia, as the chair of the forthcoming working session in Jakarta in July 1996, was given the daunting task of developing criteria for future ARF membership. The United States in particular had questioned the way in which India's claim to participation had been addressed and taken for granted by ASEAN alone. India's participation in the ARF, however, as well as that of Myanmar, was conceded by the non-ASEAN states and then endorsed by a meeting of ARF senior officials in Yogyakarta in early May 1996. This meeting also endorsed general criteria for a state's participation in the Forum based on its relevance to regional security and its political commitment. This effectively meant a moratorium on further participation, with the exception of North Korea. The ARF's diplomatic energies, however, could well be dissipated by the diluting and complicating effects of expansion at the expense of strengthening the inter-sessional dialogue activity to influence the climate of regional relations along the lines of the ASEAN model. Moreover, Myanmar's participation is almost certain to be controversial given the mixed reactions of ARF members to the repression by Yangon's military regime of its political opponents in late May 1996.

The difficulty that ASEAN faces in seeking to reconcile expanding its strategic horizons through the ARF while retaining its proprietary position, especially within South-east Asia, was exemplified by the reaction of the major powers to another initiative taken at the Bangkok ASEAN heads of government meeting in December 1995.' After more than a decade of intra-mural negotiations, a treaty was signed purportedly to create a nuclear-weapons-free zone within South-east Asia. The terms of the treaty prohibited manufacturing, storing and testing nuclear weapons, while giving individual signatories the right to grant access to the naval vessels and military aircraft of nuclear powers. The treaty also set out geographic terms of reference for regional signatories beyond their land boundaries, including exclusive economic zones and continental shelves. In addition to securing the endorsement of all the regional governments represented in Bangkok, it was also intended to attract the support of the permanent members of the United Nations Security Council. This would confer international legitimacy on the treaty, despite its primarily symbolic significance.

Here ASEAN ran into difficulty, as the United States and China, the two key powers within the ARF, raised objections. The US expressed concern that the terms of the treaty might impede the free movement of its military aircraft and naval vessels, including submarines, within the region. Indeed, in May 1995, the US had indicated a slight change in its stance over the Spratly Islands dispute by registering its fundamental interest in maintaining freedom of navigation in the South China Sea. For its part, China interpreted the treaty as being likely to prejudice its sovereign claims within the South China Sea. This negative response placed ASEAN in a dilemma given its concern to draw China into a structure of dialogue that would make it a cooperative regional partner and not an adversary. Any willingness, however, to accommodate China, in particular by modifying the terms of the treaty in its sole interest, would have caused dissension within the Association. It would also have conceded to China a regional entitlement in direct conflict with ASEAN's proprietary position. All in all, the treaty, which was not required to respond to any immediate nuclear threat, had exposed the measure of contradiction in ASEAN's regional purpose. That contradiction was also highlighted by a bilateral initiative by two ARF members, one of which was also the pivotal member of ASEAN.

As the ASEAN heads of government meeting opened in Bangkok in December 1995, Indonesia and Australia jointly announced the conclusion of a bilateral security agreement which had the status of a treaty. The existence of such an agreement raised questions about the efficacy of multilateral security arrangements based on the ASEAN model. The Indonesian–Australian accord, which had the spirit of an alliance, stated *inter alia* that the two states would consult 'in the case of adverse challenges to either party or to their common security interests and, if appropriate, consider measures which might be taken either individually or jointly and in accordance with the processes of each party'.[1] Interestingly, the agreement was concluded in the utmost secrecy. Indonesia's regional partners within ASEAN were not privy to the accord and were only informed and briefed after the event. Moreover, it appeared that even Indonesia's Foreign Ministry had not been party to the negotiations. Foreign Minister Ali Alatas was acutely embarrassed at having to face journalists in Bangkok armed only with an Australian press briefing.

Australia and Indonesia were founder members of the ARF, and Indonesia had played a key role in the formation of ASEAN. Their bilateral security agreement, given the timing of its announcement, could be interpreted as a blatant snub to ASEAN and, by extension, to the ARF which was modelled on ASEAN. Australia, an early enthusiast for a multilateral cooperative approach to regional security, had been one of the countries most frustrated by ASEAN's insistence on diplomatic centrality within the ARF. For its part, given its size, population and resources, Indonesia had at times found ASEAN too constricting a diplomatic framework within which to fulfil its regional vision. On the other hand, Indonesia felt less than comfortable within the ARF because of the country's evident lesser importance compared to the US, China and Japan.

The Indonesian–Australian bilateral security agreement may, of course, also be interpreted much more positively as complementing both ASEAN and the ARF. Indeed, all the other ASEAN states had carried over their bilateral and multilateral security agreements on entry into the Association and the ARF. For example, it had been made abundantly clear from the outset that the ARF was not an alternative to the long-standing bilateral security relationship between the US and Japan. There was some sense, however, that the Australian–Indonesian security agreement had a special significance that reflected negatively on the utility of the new multilateralism.

For Australia, the agreement made good geopolitical sense as an instrument for managing relations with its closest and most important neighbour. Nor was it a break with past practice – the ANZUS agreement, despite New Zealand's denial of facilities to the US over Washington's refusal to declare the presence of nuclear weapons on its naval vessels, had long been an important source of security cooperation with the US. For Indonesia, however, the break with principle and traditional foreign policy was striking, despite its attempts to play down the alliance quality of the agreement. Indonesia had been one of the pioneers of non-alignment and had also pushed hard for the treaty on a nuclear-weapons-free zone as a step towards making South-east Asia a ZOPFAN. Moreover, Indonesia had taken particular pride in securing the chair of the Non-Aligned Movement between 1992–95. Indeed, its tenure as chair had been trumpeted as one of the culminating triumphs of President Suharto's long rule. In one respect, the conclusion of the December 1995 security agreement with Australia may be regarded as the most significant break with the central tenet of Indonesian foreign policy since the late President Sukarno embarked on his ill-fated axis with China in the mid-1960s. The key question is what motivated Indonesia's action, which was essentially a presidential decision based, in part, on remarkably good personal relations between President Suharto and Australia's former Prime Minister, Paul Keating.

China's new-found strategic latitude and power is also believed to have played an important part in Indonesia's change of course. China's rising power as a consequence of its successful economic modernisation disturbed a number of the regional states that had encouraged the ARF's formation. Any expectation that the ARF itself might fulfil the role of the balance of power by non-military means were dashed by China's rigid and adamant adherence to its irredentist agenda in the South China Sea. Indonesia, as a state with no territorial claims in that Sea, had sought to convene an informal workshop as a way of defusing the issue through preventive diplomacy. But the stance taken by the Chinese representatives was not at all encouraging.[2] China had also appeared to lay claim to maritime jurisdiction within Indonesia's exclusive economic zone, extending from Indonesia's possession of the Natuna Islands on the western periphery of the South China Sea. A visit to Beijing in July 1995 by Indonesian Foreign Minister Alatas achieved nothing on this issue beyond the affirmation that China did not contest Indonesia's sovereignty over those islands. This equivocation on China's part, which was seen as threatening Indonesia's natural gas resources in the waters around the Natunas, expedited the conclusion of the Indonesian–Australian security agreement which had been under discussion for some two years.

The bilateral security agreement did not in itself repudiate the ARF process, but it did point to the intrinsic limitations of the ASEAN model of regional security that the Forum had adopted, at least in the first phase of its operations. The ASEAN model conspicuously avoided the problem of power by addressing regional security on a cooperative basis. As noted above, the ASEAN model was predicated on approaching security through political means alone, while permitting its members to continue with existing complementary balance-of-power arrangements outside ASEAN according to their individual circumstances. Indeed, Indonesia had been most insistent on such an approach, expressly underpinned by the presumed relationship between national and regional resilience. In entering into a security agreement with Australia, Indonesia had dipped its toes into the waters of the balance of power, albeit with no obvious sense of dependence because Australia could be portrayed as the junior defence partner. Nonetheless, Indonesia was concerned about the utility of the ARF process in its undeclared role of seeking to restrain China's regional assertiveness. The bilateral agreement with Australia was not exactly a major undertaking in securing access to an external countervailing power, but it was an evident revision of the traditional foreign policy on which both the ASEAN model and the ARF had been predicated. Moreover, it had been entered into by the very ASEAN government which, as the incumbent chair of the Standing Committee, had formal responsibility for overseeing the next stage in the institutional evolution of the ASEAN Regional Forum.

V. THE MERITS OF MULTILATERALISM

The ASEAN Regional Forum is an embryonic venture in multilateralism within a region that exists more as a category of convenience than as a coherent framework for inter-governmental cooperation. The ARF was established at a critical historical juncture as one global pattern of power gave way to another, which has yet to be clearly defined. The ARF is unique in that the formal initiative and organisational responsibility for its creation were assumed by a grouping of lesser states – ASEAN – rather than by the major regional powers. These major powers, for the time being, appear tolerant of the present arrangement which has not yet come into serious conflict with their individual interests.

Indeed, the prime object of the ARF, which ASEAN has sought to base on its own distinctive practice and experience, has been to promote stable relationships between those major powers in the general regional interest. A remarkable economic dynamism, from which all states wish to benefit further and which has been perceived positively as a hostage to the political fortunes of security dialogue and interdependence, has underpinned the new multilateralism.

The ARF, however, can be seen as an imperfect diplomatic instrument for achieving regional security goals in that it seeks to address the problem of power which arises from the anarchical nature of international society without provision for either collective defence or conventional collective security. Moreover, the degree of cooperative association the ARF has attained so far has not reduced military competition in the form of regional arms procurements. Arms procurements by a number of regional states, made possible by their astounding rates of economic growth, demonstrate the extent to which governments are unwilling to rely solely on diplomatic instruments to protect their vital interests.[1] That said, however, there is a conspicuous absence of a regional constituency for moving beyond individual force modernisation towards multilateral defence cooperation. This absence stems from a number of factors, but above all from the judgement that the traditional instrument of balance of power, if expressed in a new multilateral form, is more likely to provoke than to protect, particularly regarding China.

The problem for which the ARF is an ambitious and unproven solution is hardly new in international relations. It is that of a changing balance or distribution of power and, in particular, of the emergence of a rising power with a revisionist agenda. In the past, the emergence of such powers has invariably been associated with periods of great international turbulence, such as Asia-Pacific during the 1930s and early 1940s when Japan sought its place in the sun through militarism. The rising power in Asia-Pacific as the twenty-first century approaches is China, whose leaders harbour a historical resentment of national humiliations inflicted on their weakened state by a rapacious West. China's successful post-Cold War economic reforms have provided it with a historic opportunity to realise a sense of national destiny, which many regional states view with apprehension. The analogy with Japan does not apply in quite the same way, however, because China has not been excluded from the international economy. On the contrary, it has modernised its economy by opening up to the capitalist world, including that of the Asia-Pacific, which has reciprocated by opening up to China. In addition, there are no longer any similar revisionist states of global significance with which China could ally in challenging world order, as Japan did with Nazi Germany.

China has been welcomed into APEC and has accepted the separate memberships there of Taiwan and Hong Kong, albeit with a special status, although China's participation in the new World Trade Organisation (WTO) would seem more problematic. The United States has been at serious odds with China, particularly after the 1989 Tiananmen Square massacre, over human rights, arms and arms-technology transfers, trade and intellectual property issues and, most recently, over the highly contentious issue of Taiwan. The US has opted, however, for a policy of comprehensive yet conditional engagement, even if to Beijing that phrase is a euphemism for a new containment.[2] Despite heated differences over Taiwan, China is not being excluded from access to natural resources, capital, technology and markets, as was Japan in the 1930s. This was a critical factor in precipitating the Pacific War in 1941. Moreover, the United States no longer has the hegemonic power to interpose itself between China and interested and eager trading and investment partners in East Asia.

East Asia's governments have no interest in seeing the increasingly integrated pattern of trade and investment in the region disrupted as a consequence of their involvement in a military coalition to contain China. Such a policy is widely regarded not only as impractical on military grounds, but also as potentially highly provocative and destabilising. That judgement has not, however, been made by taking China's assurances of peaceful and good regional intent at face value. It is based instead on highly pragmatic reasoning about what is possible in the current uncertain circumstances in which the regional distribution of power continues to change and in which the region's states have less than full confidence in the ability of the US to sustain a countervailing role to prevent territorial change by force.[3]

Although the ARF is a highly imperfect diplomatic instrument for coping with the new and uncertain security context, there is no practical multilateral alternative available, at least for the time being. ASEAN's limited experience has produced only mild optimism that it may be able to transpose its model for managing regional security onto a wider regional plane with some stabilising effect. ASEAN has never sought to resolve a regional conflict. Doing so would have tested its very viability because member governments would have been obliged to take sides in the competing cases and causes of their regional partners. Similarly, the ARF has not been set up to address specific conflicts. If it had been, it is most unlikely that China would have participated. Indeed, engaging China through the ARF has been ASEAN's strongest card in sustaining its central diplomatic role. The undeclared aim of the ARF is to defuse and control regional tensions by generating and sustaining a network of dialogues within the overarching framework of its annual meetings, while the nexus of economic incentive works on governments irrevocably committed to market-based economic development.

The issue of the South China Sea disputes is a test case for the ARF's viability and efficacy to the extent that the Beijing government understands that any further Chinese assertiveness there would damage its relationship with ASEAN in particular, which it has come to regard as helpful over its other more pressing problems, especially Taiwan. Thus, China seems to have drawn a line under the Mischief Reef incident, at least for the time being, and has not allowed itself to be provoked by Philippines naval vessels destroying Chinese markers on other unoccupied reefs and atolls. This does not mean that China has given up its claims to sovereignty in the Sea, which it reiterates as indisputable and irrefutable, but it does now appear willing to tolerate the status quo, however unpalatable this is in nationalist terms. In April 1996, the Beijing government proposed that it should join ASEAN in issuing a declaration of common principles for maintaining good relations. Significantly this was linked to the ASEAN members' willingness to reaffirm a 'one China policy'. In the following month, however, a different signal was given as the Standing Committee of China's National People's Congress decided to ratify the UNCLOS and in so doing claimed an increase in maritime jurisdiction from 370,000 to 3,000,000 square kilometres.

China defined its maritime base lines for its mainland and for the Paracel Islands, but, pointedly, not for the Spratly Islands.[4]

What has been the extent up to now of the ARF's contribution in promoting 'a predictable and constructive pattern of relationships in the Asia-Pacific'? The answer at this juncture can only be a marginal one. Annual meetings of 21 and possibly more foreign ministers, and a limited number of inter-sessional activities on safe subjects, hardly constitute a new architecture for Asia-Pacific security. Such a multilateral structure is precluded from addressing the Taiwan issue as any attempt to do so in current circumstances would oblige China to withdraw from the ARF. The Forum has sought to address the Korean conflict, but has done little more than engage in well-meaning but bland comment. It has assumed no responsibility whatsoever for managing nuclear proliferation on the peninsula. The ARF has also only touched the surface of arms control, without any substantive progress on the issue of arms registers, either universal or regional, or on the issue of defence white papers.[5] The ARF, as an annual occasion, appears to have had some moderating influence on China's assertiveness in the South China Sea, but not necessarily through any intrinsic institutional qualities, so far. China has been willing to put its assertiveness on hold to engage in a united front strategy with ASEAN as a tacit diplomatic partner to resist pressures from the US and Japan.

Such tactical constraint by China is recognised for what it is worth within the rest of the Asia-Pacific, as is Beijing's unwillingness to compromise on matters of sovereignty during a transition in political leadership. This is also linked to the emotive nationalist issue of reunification with Taiwan. Although China has trumpeted the underlying economic advantages of a stable regional order, Singapore's Senior Minister, Lee Kuan Yew, received a frosty response in March 1996 when he attempted to point out to Beijing the possible costs of China's military intimidation in the Taiwan Strait. In the meantime, Chinese diplomats have shown themselves to be adept at controlling the pace of the ARF's progress as a vehicle for cooperative security. This may explain China's willingness to co-chair the next ISG on confidence-building measures.

China, as the rising regional power, has attracted the most attention in exploring the merits of the new-found multilateralism in Asia-Pacific, and in the degree to which that multilateralism may be capable of inducting members into the canons of good regional citizenship. Tensions generated by China's assertiveness are not the only ones in the region, however. For example, the diplomatic row between South Korea and Japan in February 1996 over sovereignty of the Dakto or Takeshima islets in waters halfway between the two states exposed an underlying embittered relationship that was not mitigated by the ARF which, coincidentally, had held a meeting on confidence-building in Tokyo only the month before. Indonesia and Malaysia have remained deadlocked on the question of sovereign jurisdiction of the islands of Sipadan and Ligitan off the eastern coast of Borneo, while Cambodia and Vietnam have not resolved their long-standing boundary differences either.

The ARF as an expression of cooperative security is based on a model that has succeeded within South-east Asia – up to a point – because it has avoided addressing acute problems of regional security directly. Indeed the ASEAN model, as interpreted above, was never intended to resolve such issues. Instead it has been a means of improving the climate of sub-regional relations within the framework of a limited constituency, and also, importantly, in the absence of intractable conflict. To the extent that the ARF has been created in ASEAN's image, little more may be expected of it, certainly in its formative phase. On the positive side, the embryonic multilateral structure is unique to the Asia-Pacific and is also remarkable in how much it has accomplished institutionally in such a short space of time. Moreover, it is a convenient point of diplomatic contact for the major Asia-Pacific powers. For example, the US has sought to use the ARF's inter-sessional activities to promote dialogue between its senior military and their Chinese counterparts. It also values the opportunity for bilateral dialogue at foreign-minister level which might otherwise not be politically opportune.

Yet how suitable is the ARF to undertake such a regional diplomatic role? In a world without common government, multilateral diplomacy, even when underpinned by economic advantage, suffers inevitably from intrinsic defects. In some circumstances, it may be a valuable adjunct to the workings of the balance of power in helping to deny dominance to a rising regional power with hegemonic potential. In the presence of a powerful revisionist state and in the absence of such a viable balance, expressed as a stable distribution of power, diplomacy, especially of the multilateral variety, can be very weak. Multilateral mechanisms like the ARF may work well in the presence of such a balance, but are not inherently capable of creating one.

Indeed, the prerequisite for a successful ARF may well be the prior existence of a stable balance of power. The central issue in the case of the ARF is whether, in addition to diplomatic encouragement for a culture of cooperation driven partly by economic interdependence, the region shows the makings of a stable, supporting balance or distribution of power that would allow the multilateral venture to proceed in circumstances of some predictability. The ARF's structural problem is that its viability seems to depend on the prior existence of a stable balance, but it is not really in a position to create it.[6]

The balance of power in the Asia-Pacific has been left primarily to the United States to uphold. This is still regarded in the region as somewhat problematic, despite assurances from the Pentagon and the resolve demonstrated by President Clinton and his advisers in responding to China's act of military intimidation against Taiwan in March 1996.[7] That military intimidation highlighted the utility of the US–Japanese security relationship, reaffirmed when Clinton visited Tokyo in April 1996, as well as the commitment to retain 100,000 US troops in East Asia. However, the collateral decision to return ten military installations on Okinawa to Japanese jurisdiction in response to popular opposition to the US military presence there has also raised regional concerns about whether 'America has the stamina to maintain the balance of power in the region'.[8] This concern was also reinforced by the agreement between President Clinton and Prime Minister Ryutaro Hashimoto that Japan's regional role under the security treaty should be expanded, as well as apprehension over what form that role might take.[9] Underlying uncertainty about the longer-term position of the US has encouraged regional states to make individual security provision in the form of arms procurements which threaten to start a competitive interactive trend. Uncertainty over US intentions is also linked to the ARF's ability to make practical progress in promoting concrete confidence-building measures which could help to sustain Washington's interest in the region. A proposal for a new forum for Asia-Pacific defence ministers made by US Secretary of Defense William Perry in late May 1996 suggests some frustration on Washington's part with the ARF process.

The ARF is an instrument of regional security policy, but no state would be willing to rely for its security on the Forum's ministrations alone. The ARF should be seen as serving a one-dimensional purpose only for regional states facing an uncertain security environment, but not necessarily an immediate external threat. To that extent, the ARF is a complementary diplomatic activity of the same nature as ASEAN and subject to the very same intrinsic limitations. Its initial record would not seem to support the tentative conclusion that 'what is evolving might be a distinct [sic] form of multilateralism linked to alternative understandings of the roots of conflict and ways to manage them'.[10] The ARF is certainly distinctive in its novelty and scope within the Asia-Pacific. But its promising performance has not so far demonstrated any alternative modes of conflict management, based on so-called alternative understandings of the roots of conflict, that reveal a distinctive way of accomplishing a stable regional order as pioneered by ASEAN.

To question whether the ARF is actually capable of solving problems and conflicts would be to make a category mistake. The ARF's limited objective is to improve the climate in which regional relations take place in the hope that bilateral and multilateral problems may be easier to manage. This, up to a point, has been ASEAN's experience and achievement.[11] The ARF's workings are informed knowingly or not by neo-functionalist assumptions that an incremental linear process of dialogue can produce a qualitative improvement in political relationships along the lines of the ASEAN experience. More consciously, it has been suggested that cultural tradition in the Asia-Pacific can facilitate greater regional security cooperation.[12] The fact of the matter, however, is that the ARF is an embryonic, one-dimensional approach to regional security among states of considerable cultural and political diversity and thus suffers from the natural shortcomings of such an undertaking. To interpret its role in terms of a new paradigm in international relations would be the height of intellectual naivety. It is more realistic to regard the Forum as a modest contribution to a viable balance or distribution of power within the Asia-Pacific by other than traditional means. Those means are limited, however, and the multilateral undertaking faces the same order of difficulty as the biblical Hebrew slaves in Egypt who were obliged to make bricks without straw. A constituency for any alternative form of security cooperation does not exist in the Asia-Pacific. But that does not change the nature of the ASEAN Regional Forum or its degree of relevance for coping with post-Cold War problems of regional security. The issue of relevance is reinforced by ASEAN's insistence on retaining the central diplomatic role in the ARF which confuses power and responsibility and generates frustration among North-east Asian and Pacific participants.

For the time being, it may be said on behalf of the ARF that bricks made without straw are better than no bricks at all. In the absence of any alternative set of multilateral security arrangements for the Asia-Pacific, the ARF provides a helpful point of diplomatic contact and dialogue for the region's major powers on which the prospects for stability and order depend. The continuing interest and participation of the United States, Japan and China, albeit for mixed reasons, sustain the momentum and constructive course of multilateralism. The challenge facing the ASEAN Regional Forum is how to develop and deepen the dialogue process among its expanding membership so that ASEAN's model and experience as a vehicle for conflict avoidance and management may be replicated with some tangible effect in the interest of a wider regional order.

NOTES

Introduction

[1] For analyses of ASEAN's role, see Amitav Acharya, *A New Regional Order in South-East Asia: ASEAN in the Post-Cold War Era*, Adelphi Paper 279 (London: Brassey's for the IISS, 1993); Tim Huxley, *Insecurity in the ASEAN Region* (London: Royal United Services Institute for Defence Studies, 1993); Donald Emmerson and Sheldon W. Simon, 'Regional Issues in Southeast Asian Security: Scenarios and Regimes', *NBR Analysis*, vol. 4, no. 2, July 1993; and the special issue on 'ASEAN in the Post-Cold War Era', *The Pacific Review*, vol. 8, no. 3, 1995.

[2] For a comprehensive discussion of the respective merits of regionalism, see Muthiah Alagappa, 'Regionalism and Conflict Management: A Framework for Analysis', *Review of International Studies*, vol. 21, no. 4, October 1995. See also, Louise Fawcett and Andrew Hurrell (eds), *Regionalism in World Politics* (Oxford: Oxford University Press, 1995).

[3] For differing discussions of that security context, see Barry Buzan and Gerald Segal, 'Rethinking East Asian Security', *Survival*, vol. 36, no. 2, Summer 1994, and James L. Richardson, 'Asia-Pacific Security: What are the Real Dangers?', in Coral Bell (ed.), *Nation, Region and Context* (Canberra: Strategic and Defence Studies Centre, Australian National University, 1995).

Chapter I

[1] See George McT. Kahin, *Intervention: How America Became Involved in Vietnam* (New York: Alfred A. Kopf, 1986), and Paul M.

Kattenburg, *The Vietnam Trauma in American Foreign Policy, 1945–75* (New Brunswick, NJ, and London: Transaction Books, 1980).

[2] See Leszek Buszynski, *Gorbachev and Southeast Asia* (London and New York: Routledge, 1992).

[3] See Michael Leifer, 'The Indochina Problem', in T. B. Millar and James Walter (eds), *Asian-Pacific Security After the Cold War* (Canberra: Allen and Unwin, 1993), and Carlyle A. Thayer, *Beyond Indochina*, Adelphi Paper 297 (Oxford: Oxford University Press for the IISS, 1995).

[4] For a recent account of Japan's security interests and policy in Asia, see Wolf Mendl, *Japan's Asia Policy* (London and New York: Routledge, 1995).

[5] For a discussion of the relationship between China's economic progress and regional security, see Gerald Segal and Richard H. Yang (eds), *Chinese Economic Reform: The Impact on Security* (London and New York: Routledge, 1996). See also David Shambaugh, 'Growing Strong: China's Challenge to Asian Security', *Survival*, vol. 36, no. 2, Summer 1994.

[6] See George Modelski (ed.), *SEATO: Six Studies* (Melbourne: F. W. Cheshire, 1962), and Leszek Buszynski, *SEATO: The Failure of an Alliance Strategy* (Singapore: Singapore University Press, 1983).

[7] See J. G. Starke, *The ANZUS Treaty Alliance* (Melbourne: Melbourne University Press, 1965), Jacob Bercovitch (ed.), *ANZUS in Crisis: Alliance Management in International Affairs* (Basingstoke: Macmillan, 1988), and Michael Pugh, *The ANZUS Crisis: Nuclear Visiting and Deterrence* (Cambridge: Cambridge University Press, 1989).

[8] See Chin Kin Wah, *The Defence of*

Malaysia and Singapore (Cambridge: Cambridge University Press, 1983), and 'The Five Power Defence Arrangements: Twenty Years After', *The Pacific Review*, vol. 4, no. 3, 1991.

[9] See Dick Wilson, *The Neutralization of Southeast Asia* (New York: Praeger, 1975), Heiner Hanggi, *ASEAN and the ZOPFAN Concept* (Singapore: Institute of Southeast Asian Studies, 1991), and Muthiah Alagappa, 'Regional Arrangements and International Security in Southeast Asia: Going Beyond Zopfan', *Contemporary Southeast Asia*, vol. 12, no. 4, March 1991.

[10] For an analysis of that treaty, see C. P. F. Luhulima, 'ASEAN's Security Instrument: The Treaty of Amity and Cooperation in Southeast Asia', in Kao Kim Hourn (ed.), *Cambodia in ASEAN* (Phnom Penh: Cambodian Institute for Cooperation and Peace, 1995).

[11] See Alagappa, 'Regional Arrangements and International Security', p. 292.

[12] Tan Sri Ghazali Shafi, 'Politics in Command', *Far Eastern Economic Review,* 22 October 1992.

[13] Henry A. Kissinger, *A World Restored* (New York: Grosset and Dunlap, 1964), Carsten Holbraad, *The Concert of Europe* (London: Longman, 1970), and Ian Clark, *The Hierarchy of States* (Cambridge: Cambridge University Press, 1989), ch. 6.

[14] For accounts of Indonesia's foreign policy, see Michael Leifer, *Indonesia's Foreign Policy* (London: George Allen and Unwin, 1983), and Leo Suryadinata, *Indonesia's Foreign Policy Under Suharto* (Singapore: Times Academic Press, 1996).

[15] For a summary account of intra-ASEAN territorial disputes, see Acharya, *A New Regional Order in South-east Asia*, pp. 30–37.

[16] Jusuf Wanandi, 'Security Issues in the ASEAN Region', in Karl D. Jackson and M. Hadi Soesastro (eds), *ASEAN Security and Economic Development* (Berkeley, CA: University of California Press, 1984), p. 305.

[17] For a list of Australian military exercises with ASEAN states, see Desmond Ball and Pauline Kerr, *Presumptive Engagement: Australia's Asia-Pacific Security Policy in the 1990s* (St Leonards, New South Wales: Allen and Unwin, 1996), Appendix 4.

[18] See Michael Leifer, *ASEAN and the Security of South-East Asia* (London and New York: Routledge, 1989 and 1990).

[19] ASEAN's current dialogue partners are: Australia, Canada, the European Union, India, Japan, New Zealand, South Korea, the United Nations Development Programme and the United States. It is anticipated that China will be added to the list by the end of 1996.

[20] See Mark J. Valencia, *China and the South China Sea Disputes*, Adelphi Paper 298 (Oxford: Oxford University Press for the IISS, 1995), and Michael Leifer, 'Chinese Economic Reform and Security Policy: The South China Sea Connection', *Survival*, vol. 37, no. 2, Summer 1995.

[21] See Lee Lai To, 'Defusing Rising Tension in the Spratlys: An Analysis of the Workshops on Managing Potential Conflicts in the South China Sea', *The American Asian Review*, vol. 13, no. 4, Autumn 1994.

[22] Chairman's Statement, ASEAN Post-Ministerial Conferences, Senior Officials Meeting, Singapore, 20–21 May 1993.

Chapter II

[1] Singapore Declaration of 1992, ASEAN Heads of Government Meeting, Singapore, 27–28 January 1992, p. 2.

[2] The initial membership was, in alphabetical order: Australia, Brunei, Canada, China, the European Community/Union, Indonesia, Japan, Laos, Malaysia, New Zealand, Papua New Guinea, the Philippines, Russia, Singapore, South Korea, the United States, Thailand and Vietnam.

[3] For a summary of steps leading to the formation of the ARF, see Ball and Kerr, *Presumptive Engagement*, pp. 15–25.

[4] For accounts of the circumstances and limited institutional experience of ASA, see Bernard Gordon, *Towards Disengagement in Asia* (Englewood Cliffs, NJ: Prentice-Hall, 1969), and Arnfinn Jorgensen-Dahl, *Regional Organization and Order in South-East Asia* (London: Macmillan, 1982).

[5] See Michael Leifer, 'Vietnam's Foreign Policy in the Post-Soviet Era: Coping with Vulnerability', in Robert S. Ross (ed.), *East Asia in Transition. Towards a New Regional Order* (New York: M. E. Sharpe, 1995), and Richard K. Betts, 'Vietnam's Strategic Predicament', *Survival*, vol. 37, no. 3, Autumn 1995.

[6] See *A Time for Initiative. Proposals for the Consideration of the Fourth ASEAN Summit* (Jakarta: ASEAN Institutes of Strategic and International Studies, 1991).

[7] The full text of his speech may be found in *Diplomatic Blue Book 1991*, Ministry of Foreign Affairs, Tokyo, 1992, pp. 463–71.

[8] See Yoshihide Soeya, 'The Evolution of Japanese Thinking and Policies on Cooperative Security in the 1980s and 1990s', in *Australian Journal of International Affairs*, vol. 48, no. 1, May 1994. For an official statement of Japan's security policy, see *Defense of Japan 1995*, Defense Agency, Tokyo, 1995.

[9] The current members of APEC are: Australia, Brunei, Canada, Chile, China, Hong Kong, Indonesia, Japan, South Korea, Malaysia, Mexico, New Zealand, Papua New Guinea, the Philippines, Singapore, Taiwan, Thailand and the United States.

[10] *The East Asian Miracle* (Oxford: Oxford University Press for the World Bank, 1993).

[11] For a discussion of the timeliness of the ARF, see Khong Yuen Foong, 'Predicting the Future of the ASEAN Regional Forum', *Trends*, no. 47, Institute of Southeast Asian Studies, Singapore, 30–31 July 1994.

[12] *The Straits Times*, Singapore, 26 July 1993.

[13] For discussion and advocacy of such overlapping terms, see Geoffrey Wiseman, 'Common Security in the Asia-Pacific Region', *The Pacific Review*, vol. 5, no. 1, 1992; David Dewitt, 'Common, Comprehensive and Cooperative Security, *ibid.*, vol. 7, no. 1, 1994; and Andrew Mack and Pauline Kerr, 'The Evolving Security Discourse in the Asia-Pacific', *The Washington Quarterly*, vol. 18, no. 1, Winter 1995. See also Peter Lawler, 'The Core Assumptions and Presumptions of "Cooperative Security"', in Stephanie Lawson (ed.), *The New Agenda for Global Security: Cooperating for Peace and Beyond* (St Leonards, New South Wales: Allen and Unwin, 1995), ch. 2.

[14] For a full text of his speech, see BBC Summary of World Broadcasts, FE/1589 A2/1-4.

[15] See James A. Baker, 'America in Asia', *Foreign Affairs*, vol. 70, no. 5, Winter 1991–92.

[16] *The Straits Times*, Singapore, 23 July 1993.

[17] For a discussion of the merits of a concert of powers in Asia-Pacific 'over and above the ARF', see Amitav Acharya, 'An Asia-Pacific Concert of Powers', *Trends*, no. 63, Institute of Southeast Asian Studies, Singapore, 25–26 November 1995.

Chapter III

[1] *The Straits Times*, Singapore, 26 July 1993.

[2] ASEAN Regional Forum, Chairman's Statement, the First Meeting of the ASEAN Regional Forum (ARF), Bangkok, 25 July 1994, p. 1. The text of the Chairman's Statement may be found in Sarasin Viraphol and Werner Phennig (eds), *ASEAN–UN Cooperation in Preventive Diplomacy* (Bangkok: Ministry of Foreign Affairs, 1995), pp. 258–59.

[3] Australian Paper on Practical Proposals for Security Cooperation in the Asia Pacific Region, commissioned by the 1993 ASEAN-PMC SOM, Canberra, April 1994.

[4] For the full text of his statement, see 'Opening Statement by His Excellency Professor S. Jayakumar, Minister for Foreign Affairs and Law of Singapore' at the 27th ASEAN Ministerial Meeting, Bangkok, 22 July 1994, Ministry of Foreign Affairs, Singapore, 1994.

[5] In the light of that comment, it is interesting to note the prescient suggestion by Geoffrey Wiseman writing in 1991 that 'existing ASEAN mechanisms combined with skilful statescraft could place its member states in the driving seat of a larger forum, enabling them to have a high degree of influence on location, membership and the overall shape of the regional security agenda'.

Wiseman, 'Common Security in the Asia-Pacific Region', p. 47.

[6] For an assessment of the meeting, see Khong Yuen Foong, 'Evolving Security and Economic Institutions', in *Southeast Asian Affairs 1995* (Singapore: Institute of Southeast Asian Studies, 1995).

[7] See 'Creeping Irredentism in the Spratly Islands', IISS, *Strategic Comments*, vol. 1, no. 3, 22 March 1995.

[8] The ASEAN Regional Forum, 'A Concept Paper', 18 March 1995. This document is reprinted in Ball and Kerr, *Presumptive Engagement,* Appendix 2.

[9] See Paul Evans, 'Building Security: The Council for Security Cooperation in the Asia Pacific (CSCAP)', *The Pacific Review*, vol. 7, no. 2, 1994; and Pauline Kerr, 'The Security Dialogue in the Asia Pacific', *ibid.*, vol. 7, no. 4, 1994.

[10] ASEAN Regional Forum Chairman's Statement, Meeting of the Second ASEAN Regional Forum (ARF), Bandar Seri Begawan, 1 August 1995, p. 1. This document is reprinted in Ball and Kerr, *Presumptive Engagement*, Appendix 1.

[11] He pointed out that: 'The Chinese side advocates the development of regional cooperation in security matters in stages in the spirit of dealing with issues in ascending order of difficulty, and of seeking common ground while reserving differences. For some time to come, the countries concerned may hold preliminary informal discussions and consultations on the principles, content, scope and method of cooperation in security matters. Meanwhile, they should carry out specific activities of cooperation on which the parties have reached a consensus or which are not highly contentious, and institute some